Heroes of 1960s Motorcycle Sport

Off-Road Giants!

Volume 3

Also from Veloce Publishing –

Those Were The Days ... Series
Alpine Trials & Rallies 1910-1973 (Pfundner)
American 'Independent' Automakers – AMC to Willys 1945 to 1960 (Mort)
American Station Wagons – The Golden Era 1950-1975 (Mort)
American Trucks of the 1950s (Mort)
American Trucks of the 1960s (Mort)
American Woodies 1928-1953 (Mort)
Anglo-American Cars from the 1930s to the 1970s (Mort)
Austerity Motoring (Bobbitt)
Austins, The last real (Peck)
Brighton National Speed Trials (Gardiner)
British and European Trucks of the 1970s (Peck)
British Drag Racing – The early years (Pettitt)
British Lorries of the 1950s (Bobbitt)
British Lorries of the 1960s (Bobbitt)
British Touring Car Racing (Collins)
British Police Cars (Walker)
British Woodies (Peck)
Café Racer Phenomenon, The (Walker)
Drag Bike Racing in Britain – From the mid '60s to the mid '80s (Lee)
Dune Buggy Phenomenon, The (Hale)
Dune Buggy Phenomenon Volume 2, The (Hale)
Endurance Racing at Silverstone in the 1970s & 1980s (Parker)
Hot Rod & Stock Car Racing in Britain in the 1980s (Neil)
Last Real Austins 1946-1959, The (Peck)
MG's Abingdon Factory (Moylan)
Motor Racing at Brands Hatch in the Seventies (Parker)
Motor Racing at Brands Hatch in the Eighties (Parker)
Motor Racing at Crystal Palace (Collins)
Motor Racing at Goodwood in the Sixties (Gardiner)
Motor Racing at Nassau in the 1950s & 1960s (O'Neil)
Motor Racing at Oulton Park in the 1960s (McFadyen)
Motor Racing at Oulton Park in the 1970s (McFadyen)
Motor Racing at Thruxton in the 1970s (Grant-Braham)
Motor Racing at Thruxton in the 1980s (Grant-Braham)
Superprix – The Story of Birmingham Motor Race (Page & Collins)
Three Wheelers (Bobbitt)

Essential Buyer's Guide Series
Alfa Romeo Giulia GT Coupé (Booker)
Alfa Romeo Giulia Spider (Booker)
Audi TT (Davies)
Austin Seven (Barker)
Big Healeys (Trummel)
BMW E21 3 Series (1975-1983) (Reverente)
BMW E30 3 Series 1981 to 1994 (Hosier)
BMW GS (Henshaw)
BMW X5 (Saunders)
BSA 350 & 500 Unit Construction Singles (Henshaw)
BSA 500 & 650 Twins (Henshaw)
BSA Bantam (Henshaw)

Citroën 2CV (Paxton)
Citroën ID & DS (Heilig)
Cobra Replicas (Ayre)
Corvette C2 Sting Ray 1963-1967 (Falconer)
Ducati Bevel Twins (Falloon)
Ducati Desmodue Twins (Falloon)
Ducati Desmoquattro Twins – 851, 888, 916, 996, 998, ST4 1988 to 2004 (Falloon)
Fiat 500 & 600 (Bobbitt)
Ford Capri (Paxton)
Ford Escort Mk1 & Mk2 (Williamson)
Ford Mustang – First Generation 1964 to 1973 (Cook)
Ford RS Cosworth Sierra & Escort (Williamson)
Harley-Davidson Big Twins (Henshaw)
Hinckley Triumph triples & fours 750, 900, 955, 1000, 1050, 1200 – 1991-2009 (Henshaw)
Honda CBR FireBlade (Henshaw)
Honda CBR600 Hurricane (Henshaw)
Honda SOHC Fours 1969-1984 (Henshaw)
Jaguar E-Type 3.8 & 4.2-litre (Crespin)
Jaguar E-type V12 5.3-litre (Crespin)
Jaguar Mark 1 & 2 (All models including Daimler 2.5-litre V8) 1955 to 1969 (Thorley)
Jaguar S-Type – 1999 to 2007 (Thorley)
Jaguar X-Type – 2001 to 2009 (Thorley)
Jaguar XJ-S (Crespin)
Jaguar XJ6, XJ8 & XJR (Thorley)
Jaguar XK 120, 140 & 150 (Thorley)
Jaguar XK8 & XKR (1996-2005) (Thorley)
Jaguar/Daimler XJ 1994-2003 (Crespin)
Jaguar/Daimler XJ40 (Crespin)
Jaguar/Daimler XJ6, XJ12 & Sovereign (Crespin)
Kawasaki Z1 & Z900 (Orritt)
Land Rover Series I, II & IIA (Thurman)
Land Rover Series III (Thurman)
Lotus Seven replicas & Caterham 7: 1973-2013 (Hawkins)
Mazda MX-5 Miata (Mk1 1989-97 & Mk2 98-2001) (Crook)
Mercedes Benz Pagoda 230SL, 250SL & 280SL roadsters & coupès (Bass)
Mercedes-Benz 280-560SL & SLC (Bass)
MG Midget & A-H Sprite (Horler)
MG TD, TF & TF1500 (Jones)
MGA 1955-1962 (Crosier)
MGB & MGB GT (Williams)
MGF & MG TF (Hawkins)
Mini (Paxton)
Morris Minor & 1000 (Newell)
Moto Guzzi 2-valve big twins (Falloon)
New Mini (Collins)
Norton Commando (Henshaw)
Peugeot 205 GTI (Blackburn)
Porsche 911 (964) (Streather)
Porsche 911 (993) (Streather)
Porsche 911 (996) (Streather)
Porsche 911 Carrera 3.2 (Streather)
Porsche 911SC (Streather)
Porsche 924 – All models 1976 to 1988 (Hodgkins)
Porsche 928 (Hemmings)
Porsche 930 Turbo & 911 (930) Turbo (Streather)
Porsche 944 (Higgins)
Porsche 986 Boxster (Streather)
Porsche 987 Boxster & Cayman (Streather)

Rolls-Royce Silver Shadow & Bentley T-Series (Bobbitt)
Subaru Impreza (Hobbs)
Triumph 350 & 500 Twins (Henshaw)
Triumph Bonneville (Henshaw)
Triumph Herald & Vitesse (Davies)
Triumph Spitfire & GT6 (Baugues)
Triumph Stag (Mort)
Triumph Thunderbird, Trophy & Tiger (Henshaw)
Triumph TR6 (Williams)
Triumph TR7 & TR8 (Williams)
Vespa Scooters – Classic 2-stroke models 1960-2008 (Paxton)
Volvo 700/900 Series (Beavis)
VW Beetle (Cservenka & Copping)
VW Bus (Cservenka & Copping)
VW Golf GTI (Cservenka & Copping)

General Motorcycle Books
BMW Cafe Racers (Cloesen)
BMW Custom Motorcycles – Choppers, Cruisers, Bobbers, Trikes & Quads (Cloesen)
Bonjour – Is this Italy? (Turner)
British 250cc Racing Motorcycles (Pereira)
BSA Bantam Bible, The (Henshaw)
BSA Motorcycles – the final evolution (Jones)
Ducati 750 Bible, The (Falloon)
Ducati 750 SS 'round-case' 1974, The Book of the (Falloon)
Ducati 860, 900 and Mille Bible, The (Falloon)
Ducati Monster Bible, The (Falloon)
Fine Art of the Motorcycle Engine, The (Peirce)
From Crystal Palace to Red Square – A Hapless Biker's Road to Russia (Turner)
Funky Mopeds (Skelton)
Italian Cafe Racers (Cloesen)
Italian Custom Motorcycles (Cloesen)
Kawasaki Triples Bible, The (Walker)
Lambretta Bible, The (Davies)
Laverda Twins & Triples Bible 1968-1986 (Falloon)
Moto Guzzi Sport & Le Mans Bible, The (Falloon)
Motorcycle Apprentice (Cakebread)
Motorcycle GP Racing in the 1960s (Pereira)
Motorcycle Road & Racing Chassis Designs (Noakes)
MV Agusta Fours, The book of the classic (Falloon)
Off-Road Giants (volume 1) (Westlake)
Off-Road Giants (volume 2) (Westlake)
Scooters & Microcars, The A-Z of Popular (Dan)
Scooter Lifestyle (Grainger)
SCOOTER MANIA! – Recollections of the Isle of Man International Scooter Rally (Jackson)
Triumph Bonneville Bible (59-83) (Henshaw)
Triumph Bonneville!, Save the – The inside story of the Meriden Workers' Co-op (Rosamond)
Triumph Motorcycles & the Meriden Factory (Hancox)
Triumph Speed Twin & Thunderbird Bible (Woolridge)
Triumph Tiger Cub Bible (Estall)
Triumph Trophy Bible (Woolridge)
TT Talking The TT's most exciting era – As seen by Manx Radio TT's lead commentator 2004-2012 (Lambert)
Velocette Motorcycles – MSS to Thruxton – New Third Edition (Burris)

www.veloce.co.uk

First published in in November 2014 by Veloce Publishing Limited, Veloce House, Parkway Farm Business Park, Middle Farm Way, Poundbury, Dorchester DT1 3AR, England. Fax 01305 268864 / e-mail info@veloce.co.uk / web www.veloce.co.uk or www.velocebooks.com.
ISBN: 978-1-845847-45-6 UPC: 6-36847-04745-0

For post publication news, updates and amendments relating to this book please visit www.veloce.co.uk/ books/V4745

Heroes of 1960s Motorcycle Sport

Off-Road Giants!

Volume 3

VELOCE PUBLISHING
THE PUBLISHER OF FINE AUTOMOTIVE BOOKS

Dedication

To the memory of my mum and dad and to my big brother, Rod, who, on a bright summer's day in 1961, kickstarted a love for motorcycling.

CONTENTS

Badger Goss flying on the Greeves at Bulbarrow Hill in Dorset in 1962.

FOREWORD

BY BRIAN 'BADGER' GOSS

During what is now regarded as the 'golden age' in off-road motorcycle sport, I was lucky enough to race in scrambles for the best part of 20 years, and, thanks to the hard work of motorcycle journalist and author Andy Westlake, memories from that era can be revisited and brought alive again through his two fascinating books entitled *Off-Road Giants.* They are the result of the many hours he's spent tracking down and interviewing former scrambles stars, like the Sharp and Rickman brothers, trials aces Gordon Jackson, Chris Cullen and Ken Kendall, and tough international six-day competitors including Ken Heanes, Johnny Giles, and the American all-rounder Bud Ekins. It was a personal privilege for me to be included in the line-up in volume one, and a great honour when Andy invited me to write this foreword for another trip down memory lane. Like two of his fellow journalists and enthusiasts – Peter Howdle and Ralph Venables – before him, Andy has that ability to turn a handful of words into a story that is not just about the nuts and bolts of a particular machine, but one which brings to life the people who rode them on circuits and observed sections, and spent long, strength-sapping days in the saddle on an international six-day trial.

On a cold winter evening I will often pick up one of the previous two volumes, and, as I turn the pages, I'm instantly transported back to those far off days when virtually every summer Sunday I was racing somewhere. My travels took me to all parts of the UK, all around Europe, and as far east as Russia, but many of my fondest memories are from the West Country circuits at Giants Head, Higher Farm Wick, Bulbarrow Hill and Westbury-sub-Mendip; all now sadly lost to scrambling, but still fondly remembered by those of us who raced there, and the thousands of fans who urged us on from behind the ropes. I understand it was at the circuit on the Mendips that, at the age of eight, Andy was taken by his big brother to watch his first event, and it obviously left a big impression on the lad who now writes with such passion on the riders who became his boyhood heroes. In edited form, the pieces on all of the men and women who appear in this new book have been featured in editions of both *The Classic Motorcycle* and *Classic Dirt Bike* magazine, but here you can read their whole undiluted stories, and be captivated by another set of over 100 period photographs. Sixteen former scrambles, one- and six-day trials riders are featured, including one of our first continental 'professionals' from the 1950s, Les Archer; my great rival and one time team-mate at Greeves, Dave Bickers; the hard riding John Banks; and one of my former sponsored Maico riders, Rob Taylor. Several-time British champion Nick Thompson represents the three-wheel brigade; ex-works AMC star Bill Martin is the top one-day trials star featured; and there is a whole list of multi-talented all-rounders, like Scott Ellis, Olga Kevelos, Johnny Griffiths, and Gordon Blakeway, to keep the reader glued to the book.

It's a wonderful reminder of a glorious era in off-road sport, and I know you will all enjoy reading *Off-Road Giants Volume 3* as much as I did.

Brian 'Badger' Goss

ACKNOWLEDGEMENTS

Many thanks to all of the former stars for their help and enthusiasm in compiling these profiles and for leaving a young lad from Somerset with some wonderful memories of those carefree days from his childhood. Also to Morton's, Jill and Chris Francis (Gordon Francis archive), Don Morley, Bill Riley, Francis and Nick Custard (Ron Custard archive), Sam Haslam, Bob Light (Bill Cole archive) and to the riders themselves for providing the images from that golden era.

An unusual shot of Dave Bickers having an outing on Jeff Smith's world championship-winning BSA in 1964.

Pictured at the 1962 Gloucester Grand National, near Tirley, Scott is riding his very rapid 200cc Triumph Tiger Cub.

One of the true great all-rounders of his generation, during the 1960s there was barely a major one-day trial, national motocross, or international six-day trial where the name of Scott Ellis didn't feature in the results.

CHAPTER 1

SCOTT ELLIS – THE EXCELLENT ELLIS

When young Scott Ellis rolled up to ride Dave Langston's 350cc BSA in his first trial at Hidcote in 1955, few could have realized a star was in the making. He was still only a lad of 14, but amazingly he won the Stratford-upon-Avon event that day, and it heralded the start of a long and glittering career – a career in which Scott would not only become one of the best one-day trials riders of his generation, but also an accomplished scrambler, a winner of a gold medal in the international six-day trial, and a top contender in the British grass track championship. In 48 jam-packed seasons he earned factory rides for Ariel, Triumph, BSA, Dalesman, Puch, and Greeves, winning over 20 national trials, and he was still picking up awards in Cheshire centre events up to his eventual retirement in 2005. A detached retina and worn-out knees heralded the end of active competition, but today he is still actively involved as an organiser, and it was a great pleasure to talk to him about his long and illustrious riding career.

That Scott should become a motorcyclist is perhaps not surprising, as his father was a lifelong enthusiast. Ellis senior not only rode in trials, but also worked in the motorcycle factories of Royal Enfield, BSA Redditch, Ariel at Selly Oak, and BSA again, at both Small Heath

and Umberslade, so, understandably, Scott couldn't wait until he was old enough to ride. In fact, his first event was only four days after his 16th birthday, on a slightly unusual machine for a budding trials star.

"Although I'd ridden and won that Stratford trial back in 1955, I had to wait until '57 to ride legitimately, and my first event was not in a trial, but the Banbury run on a 1912 Triumph; a 3.5hp model which I still own today. It was a lot of fun, but I couldn't wait to get started in trials, and my first real event was the Leamington Victory five clubs trial in September '57, on dad's 350cc Royal Enfield. I recall that John Houghton won, losing three marks on his 197cc James, and I had a decent enough ride with the loss of 40 or so on the Enfield. I gradually improved though, and towards the end of my first season managed to win a first class award in the trade-supported Wye Valley event, and, against a host of top works men, finished third in the Midlands centre group trial. This got me noticed, and just after my 17th birthday I was approached by Ariel, which signed me to start my second season in the factory team alongside Gordon Blakeway, Ron Langston, and Sammy Miller."

The teenager took to the 500cc works Ariel SOX 561 like a duck to water, and during the next three years chalked up numerous awards

"TAKING ON AND BEATING THE BEST IN THE TRIALS WORLD WAS EASY COMPARED TO PASSING HIS DRIVING TEST"

Manx two-day trial on the Tiger Cub in 1964.

Isny three-day enduro in 1966 on the works Tribsa.

in all of the top line British nationals. He was also proving his worth as a useful scrambles rider on the works supported HS, but his first love was trials, and you could usually bet that if an event was won by S H Miller, then Scott Ellis would be snapping at his heals and often picking up the 500cc cup. Occasionally the tables would be turned, and on his day he was certainly the match of his illustrious team-mate, but as he told me, taking on and beating the best in the trials world was easy compared to passing his driving test.

"My dad was always extremely supportive of my career, and for several years we towed the Ariel behind our family Riley on a trailer. In the Midland centre group trials I rode for the Redditch club so as few of us had our own transport we used to club together and cram up to 25 riders and their bikes into a furniture van. As you can imagine this was great going to the trial, but not so much fun coming home after the event when all of us and the bikes were covered in mud! Later on I teamed up with Mick Bowers who took me and our bikes to events all over the UK and Europe; this lasted for quite a while, because try as I might I couldn't pass my car driving test; I failed five times before I eventually passed!"

Although passing his driving test was proving to be a major problem, picking up awards in trials was much easier, and in 1960 Scott qualified for his first British experts. The event was won by Yorkshire lad Bill Wilkinson riding on 'L' plates, but for Scott it was a watershed event, and one from which he never looked back.

"There were undoubtedly some great trials riders around, and when you rode in a national against the likes of Miller, Jackson, Blakeway, Ron Langston, and Johnny Britain it was very intimidating. It certainly gave me a different mindset when Bill Wilkinson turned up on 'L' plates and proved they were only human, and they could all be beaten."

In 1960 BSA decided to disband the Ariel works team, so Scott bought his machine and carried on successfully as a privateer. However, his talents had not gone unnoticed, and by March 1961 he was being courted by Triumph. He was invited to ride its 200cc Tiger Cub, and it didn't take long for him to notch up his first win on the little four-stroke.

"The Cub was a very different bike to the 500cc Ariel, and proved to be quite a temperamental little machine, but I loved it and immediately felt at home on it. Second time out I was third in the Cotswold Cup, and a couple of weeks later won the Kickham for my first national win. In May of that year I also went to the Highlands for my first Scottish Six Days; this was the year Gordon Jackson won with the loss of his famous dab, but I had a good ride, and managed to finish seventh on the Tiger Cub. When I left school I'd joined Austin Motors as a student apprentice, so as my course was a sandwich one – six months at college and six months at the works – I'd never been able to get the time off to go to Scotland before. It was a great event, but I was slightly disappointed not to win the best newcomer award, which was awarded to Don Smith; I'd beaten him, but I was told by the organisers that as I'd already won a national trial I was exempt!"

In the summer months Scott was still racing the HS Ariel scrambler, and also a very potent Tiger Cub that was tuned to run on dope. It was a very rapid but extremely frail little bike, and there were frequent visits to the Triumph spares department to rebuild the engine, which in the enthusiastic Ellis's hands suffered several major blow ups.

In national trials Scott was now at his best on the Tiger Cub, and

he also found time to spread his wings to the continent, where he won the Saint Cucufa trial near Paris, and competed successfully in both the Belgian and Austrian experts events. After Gordon Blakeway signed for AMC he inherited his ex-team-mates 500cc Scrambler, and also got to ride in his first international six-day trial in Czechoslovakia, although actually getting to the Eastern bloc country was not without its problems.

"During the years I rode for Triumph as a factory rider there was never any contract, and it was all done on a 'gentleman's agreement' – they supplied the bikes and the spares, and also paid all of my expenses to compete in the national and trade-supported events. In scrambles my old Ariel was long past its best, and despite my persistent nagging Triumph wouldn't allocate me another bike, and it wasn't until Gordon went to AMC did they agree to let me take over his factory twin. This was 1963, and the same year they also asked me to ride Gordon's old 350cc in the Welsh three-day, which was used as a selection test for the following September's ISDT. In addition to keeping on our time schedules we had to do all sorts of other tests, like changing a tube and replacing a throttle cable while being timed and scrutinised by an ACU official. I'd never ridden in an enduro before, but I did okay, and as a result was put forward as a candidate for the team, and later asked to go to Czechoslovakia as a reserve for the British Vase team.

"To get to Czecho' it was decided that all of the bikes would be taken in a BSA lorry driven by John Harris and Jim Sandiford – who were also riding in the event – while the rest of the riders would make it there under their own steam in cars. The truck set off before us, and all was going well until we saw it stopped on the autobahn in Germany, where Jim informed us there was a "bit of a problem" and a big end had gone. We were still miles from the Czech border, so as all the bikes were on the lorry there was no other alternative than to try to carry out some sort of repair. Johnny Giles and I got the sump off in a lay-by, while someone else went off to source some new big end shells in a nearby town. We cleaned up the big end journal the best we could and reassembled the engine, but it only did another 20 miles or so before it went bang again. 'Gilo' decided that the only course of action was to take the piston and conrod out and run the engine on five cylinders, so we spent a whole day stripping and reassembling it with a piece of leather belt strapped around the big end journal. We started it up and it sounded terrible, but at least it ran and we struggled along; after a long delay we managed to get through the Czech border control, and, covered in muck and oil, eventually arrived at the trials headquarters late on the Saturday afternoon. After such an epic trip the trial itself was fairly straightforward, but the 350cc Triumph – which was big, heavy and gutless – expired on the last day when the gearbox broke. I'd ridden it virtually flat out for five days, and was still on schedule for a silver medal, so as you can imagine I was absolutely gutted when I had to pull out on the last day."

Despite the disappointment of his retirement in the ISDT, there were plenty more one-day wins for Scott and the Tiger Cub. He was leading the 1964 Scottish until the oil pump failed, but, sadly, by this time relations between him and the Triumph management were very cool, and after four successful years he went looking for another ride.

"When it was going okay the Cub was one of the best bikes I ever rode, but it was temperamental, and it was particularly frustrating when I was leading in Scotland and the engine seized. As a result I spoke to

Grass tracking in the western centre on the 500 in 1967.

Scott on the 125cc Dalesman in the Colmore Cup, 2nd February 1969.

On the Greeves Pathfinder in the 1971 Kickham.

Brian Martin and he arranged for me to have a 350cc B40 for the Welsh three-day. It was a beautiful bike to ride, and in September I was asked to be a member of the Vase team in East Germany, where unfortunately I had to retire on day four when the gearbox broke! I had no contract to 'only ride for Triumph,' but there were ructions at Meriden, and during the rest of '64 relations between us were extremely cool."

With relations at an all-time low, Scott decided it was time to change his allegiance. After testing Brian Martin's C15, he began January 1965 as an official BSA works rider. However, there was still one victory to come on the Tiger Cub: one that left Triumph less than pleased.

"I'd entered the Vic Brittain trial January 2nd, but as no works C15 was ready I decided to ride the Cub and won the event. The Cub should have been returned to Meriden by the 31st of December, so as you can imagine Triumph were not at all happy. For the first six weeks or so I rode Brian's own bike – which carried the registration number BSA 250 – and although very different to the Cub it was a super machine. Eventually I was given my own bike – BOK 228C – but compared to Brian's it felt heavy, wide and gutless. Along with Arthur and Sid Lampkin I was now under contract with a retainer in the BSA number one team, so I had little option than to try to get it to my liking. By the time the Scottish came around I was starting to get to grips with it and was actually leading for a day, but riding between sections there was suddenly a clanging noise and I had to pull out with a shot big end."

The C15 as trialled by Brian Martin was a very different bike to the standard machine, so, with his bosses' full help and approval, Scott decided to make some radical improvements to BOK 228C.

"In addition to my trials and scrambles on a 440cc Victor, I had been trying my hand at a bit of grass tracking on a B40-engined Elstar. So, influenced by the frame design on both my old HT5 Ariel and the Elstar, I designed and made a frame for the trials bike. With Brian Martin's blessing and support the new frame was completed by early November, and first time out I won a Midland centre group trial on it. Of course, higher management at BSA had no idea of what we were doing, so when two weeks later I won the British experts the press were clambering for information on the 'new' bike. Brian had some explaining to do, and it was passed off as a BSA 'experimental' machine. Most people were happy with that, but it was frustrating because it was a fantastic machine and it would have been easy for BSA to make it. For whatever reason they decided not to, and as it was a 'one off' I used it in all of the major championship trials and kept the standard 'heavy' machine for events like the Scott time and observation trial, which was a tough and real bike breaking event."

In preparation for the 1965 ISDT, Ellis rode a B40 in both the Welsh three-day and the Isle of Man two-day events, but the six-day proper was one of the wettest on record. In torrential rain – the tail end of hurricane Betsy – Ellis survived until day four, but his hopes of an ISDT gold were thwarted once again when he was forced to retire, along with the rest of the BSA team, after the B40 ran out of sparks. He would have to wait another four years before he managed to win that elusive international six days gold medal, but in-between there were plenty of one-day trials wins, and also some memorable performances on the grass.

"Through the 1965/66 winter season I won various capacity cups and team awards in national trials, and I also had my best ride in the

Scottish. I managed to finish fourth on the 'special' C15, my team-mate Sid Lampkin won the premier and the BSA team scooped the team award. In addition to the one-day trials bike, BSA also supplied me with my ISDT mount, a 440 scrambler and all my engine spares for the Elstar grass track bikes. With plenty of spares at hand it meant we could indulge in some fairly radical tuning and on the 250 I managed to win a round of the British championships."

After the debacle of the '65 international in which all of the BSA team retired, the BSA/Triumph group decided it was going to build a bulletproof machine for the 1966 event in Sweden. They would use all of the 'good bits' from around the group, and the result was the BSA/Triumph hybrid, one of which was ridden by Scott, but following a heavy crash he was sidelined by a broken top fork yoke on the 500 twin.

1967 would be the last year for the works BSA trials team, and the Midlander decided to buy all of his factory bikes and continue as a privateer. British championship wins on his 250cc BSA-engined Antig sponsored both the one- and six-day trials, although his quest to win a gold in the international was thwarted yet again, this time in Poland when more electrical gremlins forced him out. Away from motorcycling things were going well, and on the work front Scott was promoted to manager of the prototype build department at Longbridge, and also attained chartered engineer status with the Institution of Mechanical Engineers. In 1968 he and Sue decided to get married, so restoring their house meant that the grass track winnings now bought bricks and cement. In trials he was still winning on the old C15, but a chance meeting with Peter Edmondson led to a works ride with Puch, and eventually that elusive ISDT gold medal.

"By the late '60s lightweight two-strokes were very much in the ascendancy and Peter invited me to try out the new Puch-engined Dalesman trials bike he was developing. It was a super little bike, and after picking up a few awards in local one-day trials I rode it in that year's British experts, and Peter arranged for me to have a souped-up version for the Welsh three-day. I ended up winning the trial ahead of the British team hopefuls, and on the strength of this Peter Bolton of Puch UK asked me if I was interested in riding a factory bike in the ISDT; as you can probably guess it didn't take too long to say "Yes please!" The ISDT that year was in Germany, and with a fantastic bike and superb factory backup which included my own personal minder, I came away from Garmisch with a gold medal."

Scott rode the six-speed single cylinder two-stroke in two more internationals, but the '69 event in Germany would be his only gold medal. In Spain the following year he retired with a broken gearbox, and in the Isle of Man in '71 he was on schedule for gold until the clutch fell off in the final special test, and he spent more than his allowed 15 minutes replacing it and had to settle for silver. When Greeves announced its new 170cc Puch-engined Pathfinder, Scott was the obvious man for a works ride, and over the next three years he picked up many awards on the Thundersly two-stroke. This included the 200cc cup in the Scottish Six Days, and the premier award in the Cotswold Cup. The 1972 Cotswold would be his last national win but certainly not the end of Scott Ellis' trials career.

"When Greeves packed up I was offered a Bultaco Sherpa by my local dealer, Karl Rowbottom – I think this was the first bike I'd had to buy in all my years of riding in trials – and on it I qualified for the British experts. By then Sue and I had a two-year-old daughter, so I'd given up chasing around the country riding in all of the nationals, and at the end of '74 I left Longbridge and upped sticks to take up a new job as research and development manager at JCB in Staffordshire."

Although by then not a challenger in the British championships, Scott would continue riding Bultaco, SWM, Yamaha, Honda and Beta machines up to his retirement in 2005. His career spanned a wonderful 48 years, in which he was one of the greats of his generation.

Many thanks to Scott for all his help in compiling this profile, and for some super memories of a golden era.

Bultaco-mounted in the 1972 inter-centre team trial at Burrington.

On the 250cc Dot in the Scott trial, November 1962.

In a glittering career that began on a Greeves trials bike in the winter of 1960, the big man from Bury St Edmunds went on to become one of the greatest motocrossers of his generation, and but for bad luck could have been twice-crowned world champion on his booming BSAs.

CHAPTER 2

JOHN BANKS - BARON OF ST EDMUNDS

Back in the days of the Cold War, motorcycle enthusiasts behind the Iron Curtain had little opportunity to witness international off-road sport, so it's therefore not surprising that on a hot summer's day in 1969 a crowd estimated at over 125,000 gathered for the Soviet round of the world 500cc motocross championship. The location was the hillsides near the town of Kishinev in south west Russia, and as there were few privately owned cars on the road, most of the spectators arrived with chairs and makeshift 'grandstands,' jam-packed into hundreds of old lorries, all eager to see the pick of the world's best scrambles stars in action. With dust billowing and the crackle of open exhausts filling the air, they witnessed some great racing, but at the end of a long hard day they boarded their buses and departed with few having any idea who had actually won. The race organisers didn't seem to be too keen to announce that a 'foreigner' had beaten the best of eastern Europe, and by the time the delayed presentation took place, the bulk of the crowd was gone, so only a handful witnessed works BSA man John Banks step forward to collect the winner's garland.

With the season past the halfway stage, the rider from Bury St Edmunds was now leading the championship table, and there was plenty

of optimism that if the bike remained reliable and he could maintain his impressive run of form, the BSA man could win that elusive world crown. The previous year he had been beaten to the title by a single point by East German Paul Friedrichs, so to find out more about that disappointment and how the rest of the '69 season developed, I visited John at the beautiful home he shares with his wife, Mary, in Suffolk, where we relived some of those golden days. For the best part of 20 years he raced all across the world on a variety of works Dots, BSAs, Cheneys, CCMs and Hondas, but, as he recalled, it all started on a winters day in 1960, with a Greeves trials bike. He was only a lad of 16, but he'd already earned the nickname 'the Baron' – one that would be featured in numerous headlines over the years.

"When I was a kid my dad was a builder, and because we lived in a big house all my school friends thought we were well off, so one day someone called me the Baron and it stuck throughout my racing career. When I left school I went to building college to learn the basics, and then became a plumber working for my dad, Monty; he owned several motorbikes, but unlike his namesake didn't ride in trials or scrambles, and my first insight into competition came when I was aged about 15 and met Mary. Mary's brother Roger Dutton was quite

On the works Dot at the British 250 Motocross GP, Shrubland Park, June 1963.

"HE WAS ONLY A LAD OF 16, BUT HE'D ALREADY EARNED THE NICKNAME 'THE BARON' – ONE THAT WOULD BE FEATURED IN NUMEROUS HEADLINES OVER THE YEARS"

On the works BSA at Farleigh in May 1968.

a handy scrambler – in fact, he won the eastern centre championships one year – and we used to go along to watch him race and cheer him on. Around the same time I also first met and became friends with Doug Theobold, who was starting to make his mark in local trials, so, bitten by the competition bug, I decided that as soon as I was old enough I would have a go myself. My fist bike was a Greeves Scottish which I bought from Dave Bickers, and I used to take it along to the building sites where we were working, and in the lunchtimes and evenings put in endless hours of practice riding up and down muddy slopes. Just after my 16th birthday in 1960 Doug took me and the bike in his van to my first trial in Essex, and I amazed myself by winning the novice award; better still, two weeks later we rode in a local Bury St Edmonds event in which I beat Doug and won the premier award. The funny thing was that although I continued to ride for many years in trials, it was the only event I ever won!"

With his appetite whetted it wasn't long before John was lining up in his first scramble; a memorable day in which he departed from home as a junior and returned in the evening as an expert.

"I was desperate to start scrambling, so thanks to dad I got a new 250cc Greeves which, as I was still only 16 and unable to drive a car, my brother-in-law Trevor transported in his pick-up. It was a local event – I can't remember the exact location now – but at the end of my first junior race I can vividly recall the joy of seeing the chequered flag and realising I was the winner. It was fantastic to win, but in those days if you won a junior race you instantly got upgraded to an expert, which meant the rest of that season was a pretty steep learning curve."

Along with Trevor – who doubled as race transport and mechanic – John began to broaden his racing horizons, and during that 1961 season there were numerous 250cc wins on the Greeves. With his full-on, never-say-die riding style, people began talking about the talented young Banks as a future champion, and there was little surprise when Bernard Scott-Wade invited him to start his second full season on the works Dot.

"It was a great honour to be asked to ride a works machine and they supplied me with a couple of scramblers plus a trials bike to keep me in trim during the winter. Bernard Scott-Wade and his son Michael were very good to me, but as I soon discovered there was little in the way of any money, and although the Dots handled well on rough circuits, they didn't have the speed of the Greeves, and when ridden hard they regularly broke down. That said, I managed to get a few good results, and thanks to Doug Theobold I managed to get some additional sponsorship which allowed me to do a few of the 250cc world championship rounds. I recall that for my first race I went with fellow Dot rider John Griffiths, with the bikes towed on a trailer behind my mum's Vauxhall Victor car. The journey through France was horrendous, as with the additional weight of the bikes it wouldn't pull uphill, and going down anything more than a minor slope the brakes didn't work. I recall one particular incident when we couldn't stop in time and had to dodge in and out of a petrol station to miss a large vehicle coming the other way."

Getting to and from that first motocross GP in Spain was a hair-raising experience, but on the track the Dot decided to behave and John was soon mixing it with the best quarter-litre racers in the world.

"It might sound a romantic way of life travelling around Europe racing a motorbike, but it was all done on a shoestring and I had to do all my own mechanical work on the bike. Its favourite trick was to strip gears, and I always carried some spares with me, but in the Spanish GP it ran faultlessly and I managed to bring it home in ninth place, which was very satisfying. Later on that season I managed to get some start money from the FIM, and also had my best result when I managed to finish third in the Swiss GP; as you can imagine, Bernard Scott-Wade was delighted. Over the years the Dot factory had spent little money developing or improving the engine, and all of us works-supported riders were left pretty much to our own devices to find ways of improving them. We tried all sorts of things, but the main problem was with the Villiers engine, which of course was never designed to cope with the rigours of motocross. From racing in the GPs and international events we were very much aware of how blisteringly fast and incredibly reliable the Czech CZs were, so in an effort to match them we managed to get a few engines and fitted them into the Dot rolling chassis. They showed some promise, but for whatever reason they never worked as well in the Dot as they did in a CZ, and we eventually gave up on the idea."

During the next three or four seasons John travelled to many international and world championship meetings with his friend and Greeves ace Dave Bickers in his pick-up, but by now the Dot was outclassed by the twin port CZs, and at the age of 23 he landed the perfect works ride with BSA.

"Jeff Smith had won two world titles on the BSA in 1964 and '65 so as the bikes had a winning pedigree I didn't need much persuasion when, in 1966, their competition manager, Brian Martin, invited me to join the works team. I was now a professional rider competing in all the British championship races on the B44 Victor, and the following year I also raced a 540cc bike in three rounds of the 750cc Coupe Moto Europe. My first race was in Austria, and I vividly remember the sight and sound of Sten Lundin as he overtook me on his Lito, which was like a tank compared to my BSA. Unlike my days at Dot when I had to do all my own mechanical work, all I had to do at BSA was race the bike while my mechanic – sidecar racer Norman Hanks – did a superb job keeping the engines in top fettle. The big bore 540 was a great motor, but it was hard pushed to deal with its extra ccs, and blew up in a big way at the Red Marley hillclimb. It went 'bang' and couldn't be used again. I only rode in one 500cc GP that year – the last one of the season after Jeff Smith had broken his arm – and raced the titanium-framed bike Jeff had been developing. It was a full 500 and weighed in at an incredibly light 196lb, but in the cut and thrust of racing it was a bit fragile, and if the titanium fractured it couldn't be welded like with a conventional steel frame."

John had only raced in a handful of world championship events during the tail end of '67, but his talent was there for all to see, and 1968 began in the way he hoped it would continue with a scintillating win in front of the BBC TV cameras on the 499cc Beezer. The costly titanium frame had been discarded, and the Banks mount for the new season was the lean, aggressive and extremely functional B50 Victor GP. With its nickel-plated frame (which carried the engine oil), magnesium fork sliders and wheel hubs, it weighed in ready to race at 235lb, and with an engine turning out just over 37bhp at 6000rpm it was capable of taking on and beating the world. In fact, the BSA new boy only had to wait until the French GP in July to notch up his first win, when, after finishing second to Roger de Coster in the first leg, he went one better in the second to bring the booming BSA home first ahead of Bengt Aberg on his 420cc Husqvarna for overall victory. With

Flying on the works BSA at Dodington Park in April 1968.

Torsten Hallman (33) leads John (41) at the Motocross des Nations, Farleigh, 7th June 1969.

his world championship victory duck now broken Banks was on a roll, and the following week he won both legs in the Dutch GP, followed by second overall in the Belgian round to put him in the championship lead. Throughout that memorable season John had the East German Paul Friedrichs snapping at his heals, and, despite another second overall in Luxemburg that maintained his lead, Friedrichs was only six points behind as they lined up for the final round in Switzerland. Second place in both races saw the CZ rider the overall winner, and his total points score gave him the world championship by one mark over the unlucky Banks; so near, and yet so far.

To miss a world championship by a solitary mark was a bitter pill to swallow, but there was some recompense for John, as at home the combination of Banks and the BSA was almost unbeatable, and he ran away with the 500cc British title that year. Optimistic that he could go one better, the big man from Bury St Edmonds started the 1969 season with an impressive win in the Hants GN, but, as he recalled as the season progressed, it was an almost exact repeat of the previous one.

"There was some good continental opposition for the Hants, and I was pleased to beat Geboers and Teuwissen to win the Good Friday classic. In the next months I had some good wins in both the British and world championship races – first overall in the Czechoslovakian round at Prerov, and also in the Russian event at Kishinev – and by the time we went to the Belgian round in August I was leading the world again. Sadly, that was where the rot set in. In the next race in West Germany I had to retire with ignition failure, and after I finished third in the first leg in Luxemburg I suffered a puncture in the second and had to pull out. This was very frustrating, as you had to finish both legs to win any points, so I'd then lost my championship lead, and when the ignition failed again in France I could see my chances quickly disappearing. In Switzerland I injured my wrist in practice, and then suffered another puncture in the race, and by then had slipped to third behind Friedrichs. I managed to finish fifth overall in the final round in East Germany, and, with Friedrichs retiring in the second leg, I was back up to second, but Bengt Aberg was crowned the new champion."

Although he'd been out of luck in the world rounds, Banks once again had the solace of winning his second British title in '69, and in doing so became the fourth BSA man to win the coveted crown. But as he revealed, it would be his last year of glory on the Small Heath four-stroke.

"The 1970 world championship season opened on April 11th in Switzerland, but for me it was a disaster. In the second leg I was holding a decent fourth when I fell and broke my little finger, and, although I was fit to ride in the next round in Holland, I then dislocated my knee twice in the space of five weeks and had to have an operation for torn ligaments, which put me out for the rest of the season."

However, it wasn't all gloom and doom in 1970. Over in America motocross was starting to really take off, and promoter Edison Dye arranged for a group of world championship riders to take part in the new Trans Am race series. These included John and his BSA team-mates Dave Nicoll, Keith Hickman and Jeff Smith, who all put on a super show for the huge stateside audience. Riding a mixture of 250 and 500cc bikes, the eight-round series ended in a BSA one-two-three with Nicoll, Banks and Smith heading the leader board, but, as John told me, this was just a lull before the storm that broke in the summer of 1971.

"The season started okay for us when I won a televised

international from my team-mate Dave Nicoll at Dodington Park, near Bristol, but it was obvious that things weren't good with the parent company when we started going to the GPs with a shortage of spares and things missing from the bikes. I managed to finish eighth overall in Italy, got a third in Sweden, and was third overall at Farleigh in the British GP, but at the end of the meeting we were told by a glum-faced Brian Martin that the competition department was to close down and it was our last day as BSA works riders."

Overnight the works BSA riders were out of a job, and although they were offered the continued use of their works Victors at their own expense until the season's end, along with a degree of spares as backup, only Dave Nicoll availed himself of this, and John rode the rest of the season on a 420cc Husqvarna. Although he had spent much of his racing life on big four-strokes, he took to the Husky like a duck to water, and at the end of the '71 season was once again crowned 500cc British champion. He also returned to the States, where he raced a CZ alongside Dave Bickers and Chris Horsfield, and again finished runner-up in the Trans Am series, but away from the racetracks he had opened a busy motorcycle shop in his home town of Bury St Edmonds, which proved to be a useful distraction while he pondered his motocross options.

"I'd started the bike shop in 1968 in premises my dad had previously used as a petrol station, but by 1971 we had taken on the Honda agency and moved to a purpose-built car and bike showroom just down the road. In the GPs the big BSA had been very much the lone four-stroke, but on its day it was still competitive, so after meeting with Eric Cheney I decided to race his B50-engined bike in the 500cc championship races. I also took up the offer from the Ossa importer to race one of their 250s, but the way I was 'signed' to ride for Eric was quite bizarre. He had asked me if I was 'interested in riding for him next year,' and we arranged to meet in his local pub to discuss it. I told him that I couldn't do it for nothing, and with that he got a large biscuit tin out of his bag and presented it to me. I opened it and discovered it was full of money; I think it had been stored under his bed, and it was my 'signing on' fee for the year. Eric was a great engineer, and made some good bikes which both went and handled extremely well, so I was optimistic that I could fulfil his dream of winning a 500cc GP. During the next couple of seasons I had some good rides, and almost managed it in 1973 when I split the two works Suzukis of De Coster and Wolsink and finished second at Carlsbad in America. Sadly, despite my best efforts, by then the two-strokes ruled the roost, and we never did get that elusive win."

Although the Cheney was outstripped by the lighter and faster two-strokes in the GPs, with Banks in the saddle it was still extremely competitive in the home championship, and in 1973 John scooped his fourth 500cc title; the last time it would be won by a British four-stroke. By now BSA had slipped into the abyss, but there was still plenty of motocross life left in the B50-based single, and after two eventful seasons on the Cheney he swapped camps to line up with former BSA team-mates Vic Allen and Vic Eastwood, on one of Alan Clews' very potent CCMs. 1976 was an extremely productive season for the works CCM team, with Allen second, Banks fourth and Eastwood a strong fifth in the British championship, and there were also some memorable top five finishes in the GPs. Certainly anyone who witnessed those races can still vividly recall the blood-stirring sight and sound of the three factory stars on their big bangers as they fought to keep the

John in his last GP, on the works BSA at a muddy Farleigh in July 1971.

"I TOLD HIM THAT I COULDN'T DO IT FOR NOTHING, AND WITH THAT HE GOT A LARGE BISCUIT TIN OUT OF HIS BAG AND PRESENTED IT TO ME. I OPENED IT AND DISCOVERED IT WAS FULL OF MONEY"

Trying hard on the CZ at Matchams Park in April 1972.

hordes of two-strokes at bay. Throughout his career John was known as a hard and determined rider with an aggressive 'sitting' (as opposed to a standing) racing stance, which inevitably gave his bikes a thorough pounding, and the sight of the welding gear being used on a fractured frame tube, footrest or broken seat between races was a fairly common one on his works CCM during 1976 and '77 seasons. He loved the long stroke 580cc, which was ideally suited to his low revving riding style, but he was also still able to turn in some stunning rides on the short stroke 500, including fourth place at the Canadian GP, and an inspired ride at the British round at Farleigh Castle, where he finished runner-up – a great performance on the sweet-handling CCM.

During the winter of 1978/79 the welding gear was out again – not to repair a broken frame, but to manufacture a new one which carried the name 'Merlin.'

"I was now selling both Honda bikes and cars through our shop, so I asked if they could supply me with one of the engines that were being used successfully for desert racing and motocross in America. They duly came up with a 350 assembled by Mugen – a Japanese company formed in 1973 by Masao Kimura and Hirotoshi Honda, the son of Honda motor company founder Soichiro – which we housed in a frame of my own design made by Merlin, a local company who normally produced single seater racing cars."

John's first race outing was in front of the TV cameras in an icy wintertime meeting near Southend: ideal conditions for the Honda-engined Merlin, which held a strong field at bay for an impressive debut win. Despite some initial problems with the gearbox – solved with some specially-made Quafe gears – the new bike, now a full-blown 500, proved extremely competitive, and this prompted the manufacture of 25 CCM-framed JBR 500s, which were sold through his dealership, John Banks Racing, during the summer of 1979.

The John Banks replicas would be a lasting and fitting reminder of the big man on his booming four-strokes, but as the new decade dawned he finally decided to call it a day, and his retirement brought the curtain down on 20 fantastic years of racing.

Works rider, four-time British 500cc champion, four BBC *Grandstand* trophy titles, two *World of Sport* championships, East Anglian Sports Personality of the Year, and twice runner-up in the world; not a bad record for the popular man from Bury St Edmonds, who summed it all up as follows:

"Obviously, there was the disappointment of the punctures and ignition problems which meant I lost the world championship by one point, but, that aside, I had a great career in which I rode some fantastic bikes. We went to places, like Russia, I would never have gone to, and also made many good friends along the way. It was tough travelling around Europe with two bikes and a pair of spare wheels for five weeks on the trot, but it was a wonderful life and one I wouldn't have changed for the world."

John Banks: without doubt one of the greatest scramblers of his generation.

Many thanks to John and Mary for their time and hospitality, and for some wonderful memories from a golden era.

John on the Cheney BSA leads Vic Eastwood at a dusty Leighton in July 1973.

CHAPTER 3

BILL FAULKNER – FOR THE LOVE OF THE SPORT

Though never a superstar, Bill Faulkner enjoyed many years competing on both two and three wheels, and, although his ready smile sometimes suggested he was 'taking it easy,' he was a top class performer during the golden era of one-day trials.

Once described by famous scribe Ralph Venables as being "erratically brilliant," there were few major national trials in the 1950s and '60s where the name of WGR 'Bill' Faulkner didn't figure in the results. Exceptionally good on the rocks – especially in the Highlands of Scotland, where he competed 13 times in the six-day classic – Bill was one of the trials world's great characters; a man who for over 25 years rode with a smile on his face in the sport he loved.

To find out more about his long and successful off-road career – which began on a BSA Bantam in 1952, and went on to include both one- and six-day observation trials, two memorable rides in the ISDT, the occasional outing on the scrambles track, and three eventful seasons in sidecar trials – I met up with him at the beautiful home he shares with his wife, Maureen, in rural Oxfordshire. That Bill Faulkner should have become a motorcyclist was not surprising, as from an early age the sound of bike engines and the aroma of hot oil was in his blood. He takes up the story:

"After starting out both building and selling push-bikes – called the Cardigan cycle – by 1936 my father had progressed to motorcycles, and two years later he became the BSA agent in Oxford. He competed in several prewar long distance events like the MCC's Exeter and

Land's End, and bought an ex-works BSA M24 outfit on which he had his annual outing in the local Colmore Cup national trial. When I was in my early teens I got involved in cycle speedway, but I'd been bitten by the trials bug and could hardly wait until I was 16 – no schoolboy sport in those days – and my first motorcycle. This was a new 125cc D1 Bantam which dad took from stock, and, along with my two pals Pat Lamper and Joe Johnson – who would later both become top line scramblers – I spent countless hours practising at the nearby gravel pits. My first event was a Henley-on-Thames club trial, and although I didn't win an award I had a decent ride and managed to finish exactly halfway in the results."

Although Faulkner senior was fully supportive of his son's trials career, and supplied him with the Bantam, he was – as Bill recalled – not so forthcoming when it came to giving him a job when he left school.

"During my school days I used to go down to the workshop and 'get in the way,' so when I left school it wasn't too much of a surprise when my dad told me he wouldn't employ me, and I went to the local iron works as a toolmakers apprentice for five years. I had to work a 49-hour week and they paid me £2 10s; out of that I gave my mum 30

Off-Road Giants!

bob for keep and kept the rest for myself: father said that he would pay them to have me, let alone them pay me!"

Bill rode the little BSA in quite a few closed to club and open to centre events during the winter of '52/'53, and it was this bike on which he competed in his first national, and also earned an upgrade to expert status: the latter, as he recalled, achieved in a rather bizarre manner.

"Back in the early '50s few of us had the luxury of a car and trailer, pick-up or van, so the only alternative was to ride your bike to the trial, compete, and then ride it back home again. After riding in the local Colmore Cup – our first national – Pat Lamper and I decided to spread our wings a little and have a go at the Three Musketeers regional restricted trial. I was having a pretty good ride, but following weeks of heavy rain the river sections were extremely difficult, and after a drowning in a river section the Bantam died and I had no alternative other than to retire and leave it propped up against a tree. I got a lift back to the finish to sign off, and returned the following day to rescue the bike. Imagine my surprise when a few days later the results appeared and there was my name against the best novice award. It transpired that with the light fading the organisers had decided to scrub the last few sections, which meant that because I'd lost least marks up to the section where I'd retired, I was awarded the trophy and upgraded to expert in a trial I didn't actually finish; from then on I regarded myself as 'the expert who never was.'"

After two seasons on the Bantam, Bill realised that if he was going to improve something more competitive was required. As his father was an agent for the Birmingham-made two-strokes, this came in the form of a rigid-framed 197cc Sun. During the next couple of seasons Faulkner and the Sun were regular award winners in not just the south Midlands, but also in the southern, western, Wessex and south eastern centres, the little two-stroke having undergone a series of makeovers by its resourceful rider.

"The original Sun – TJO 1 – had a rigid frame, but I think that the jig must have been made out of string because when we got bits for it nothing fitted. I was always looking for ways to improve the power delivery and handling, and over the next couple of seasons I bored out the engine to 225cc, replaced the standard MP teles with a pair of Earls leading link front forks, and Sun gave me a new swinging arm frame. To get some extra steering lock I also put some dents in the petrol tank– this was sent back to the factory for re-chroming – and for the 1956 season changed the 9E engine for the latest Villiers 10E. I think the best ride I had on that bike was in the Mitchell trial: John Brittain won with a loss of seven, his brother, Pat, was second with 12, and I won the 200cc cup with a loss of 13. During that season I'd also started riding a brand new rigid B32 350cc BSA, but it was very different to the little two-stroke, and on reflection I should have just stuck to one bike."

After his debut ride on the BSA in the '55 Scottish Six Days, Bill entered on a new B34 Springer in the following year's event, but, as he revealed, an unfortunate accident in the Cotswold Cup trial gave him the chance to ride a works Triumph Tiger Cub.

"I was riding the Sun along a narrow lane when, suddenly, John Draper and Jack Wicken – who it transpired had missed a section – came round a corner towards me. John missed me, but Jack hit my handlebars and crashed into a wall which he catapulted, leaving both him and his 500cc Triumph laid out in the field. My bike was bent and twisted, but I kicked it straight and carried on to the finish, where I

was met by a very apologetic Henry Vale, who offered to pay for any damage. I told him that I would 'give anything to ride a works Triumph,' but I heard nothing more until I arrived in Scotland the following May, where Mr Vale approached me and asked if I would like to ride the factory Tiger Cub. The bike – the first one with a swinging arm frame – was due to be ridden by George Fisher, but after a week's practice he'd gone down with food poisoning, and after Bill Martin had declined I took over his bike."

Less than two months after the collision in the Cotswold Cup, Bill joined Jack Wicken and Johnny Giles in the Triumph works team for the '56 six days, but before he got under way there were some stern words of warning from Henry Vale.

"He told me 'I don't care what you do, blow the engine up or whatever, but don't break the frame, it's the only one we've got and we're putting a 175cc engine in it next week for Ken Heanes for the selection tests at the Welsh three days.' Riding a small capacity four-stroke was all new to me, and with its small section, 3.50x18 rear tyre, and long seat it didn't handle very well and I had a fairly poor ride, but in-between dodging the sheep I had lots of fun trying to catch John Draper's 150cc Bantam across the moors. The little Triumph held together okay, but on the last day I overdid it and fell off on a roundabout. There wasn't much damage done, and I managed to ride to the finish and sign off, but the funny thing was the following week they put the 175cc motor in for Ken, and later the frame broke in the ISDT!"

It was back to the old faithful 500cc BSA for the rest of the '56 season, which saw Bill a regular award winner in all of the major nationals, including a memorable ride in the Welsh one-day, where he won a first class. On the strength of this, the following year he was signed up as an official member of the Triumph works team with a 500cc twin for the Scottish; an event that, as he recalls, also saw a race star of the future on a Triumph.

"The '57 Scottish saw all of the works men – bar me on Johnny Giles 500cc twin – on Tiger Cubs, and they also lent another Cub to Mike Hailwood. At that time Mike was working for Triumph as an apprentice, and I remember his bike turning up in one of the Kings of Oxford vans, while his dad, Stan, arrived in his white Bentley Continental. Even at the age of 17 it was obvious that he had his heart set on road racing, and he only rode the Monday and then called it a day. I had a much better ride than the previous year, and continued to use the big twin in all of the important nationals for the next six months or so, until John asked for it back and I was given another Cub. Although a bit fragile, this was a super little bike – much better than the one I'd ridden in '56 – and I took to it like a duck to water. I won quite a few awards on the 200cc single – including a first class in the West of England – but then, just before the Mitchell trial in Wales, Henry Vale told me it would be my last ride, and after the event I was to return it to the factory. I think it annoyed Henry that I always rode with a smile on my face, which he misconstrued as 'not trying,' so it didn't come as a great surprise when he told me the Mitchell was to be my last event as a Triumph works rider."

By now Bill had joined his father's burgeoning motorcycle business in Oxford, and with a typical Saturday often seeing 20 new and secondhand bikes sold, it was not, as he recalled, the day to choose to get married.

"In addition to dad and me we had five mechanics; two on servicing and repairs, while the other three concentrated on preparing

On the Sun during the 1955-56 season. The bike had been rebuilt to accommodate MP Earles forks and a swinging arm.

"BECAUSE I'D LOST LEAST MARKS UP TO THE SECTION WHERE I'D RETIRED, I WAS AWARDED THE TROPHY AND UPGRADED TO EXPERT IN A TRIAL I DIDN'T ACTUALLY FINISH"

On the works Cub at Culcross in the 1956 Scottish.

In the southern centre team trial on the works Cub in December 1957.

the new and secondhand bikes. Most Saturdays we would take eight or ten in part-exchange deals, and before we went home in the evening all of them would be steam cleaned in readiness for the mechanics to service before they appeared – all spick and span – in the showroom the following week. When Maureen and I announced we were getting married my father told us that he had no intention of shutting the shop on a Saturday, so we had to change it to Thursday."

Although Bill had lost his ride on the works Tiger Cub, he was soon mounted on another factory bike for the 1958 season; a 197cc Francis Barnett. Things began well on the Villiers-powered Barnett, but, as he recalled, it all went downhill when the Coventry firm decided to change to a new but largely untried engine, with blow ups and retirements.

"In early '58 Ernie Smith – a well-known trials and ISDT rider from pre and postwar – had taken over as competitions manager at Francis Barnett, and he offered me a 197 which I rode in a few of the early season nationals. Barnett's were changing over to the French AMC engine for their road bikes, so Ernie built one into a trials frame and promptly won the *Coventry Evening Telegraph* event on it before passing it on to me. I tested it and was very confused, because the gearbox would change four times but there were only three actual gears. We were due to go to Ireland to ride in the Hurst Cup, so on the Friday morning I went up to Coventry to strip the engine in the Francis Barnett comp shop. This was an old wooden army hut on the side of the road by the main building in Lower Ford Street, and I was amazed that everything in it – including the Sharp bothers scramblers, Ernie's wife's push-bike, and even the lawn mower – was all painted in Arden green! With the engine disassembled, it was soon discovered that two gears had been interchanged and they were cancelling each other out, but it was just the start of numerous problems that beset my AMC-engined bike. Other than the episode with the drowned Bantam, during my previous six years in trials I'd never retired, but during that season on the 250cc Barnett I packed up five times. One of these was at the Kickham, when after kicking the engine into life it ran backwards, quickly followed by a big bang and then silence when it seized solid. Arthur Browning towed me and the dead bike out of the section, and the following week I returned it to the Barnett comp shop; on stripping

the motor down, Ernie Smith's reaction was 'You've wrecked it, the only thing we can salvage is the gearbox and clutch.'"

Although it was a disappointing and frustrating season on the works Francis Barnett, there was one outstanding performance in that year's Cambrian, which earned Bill his first national win. The hard-fought victory earned him a ride in the British experts, but, as he recalled, his decision to ride his brightly painted and modified old 197cc bike didn't go down too well with Ernie Smith.

"Ernie had sent me a new tyre and some other bits and pieces, but after all of the frustrations with the AMC-engined bike I decided to ride the old 197 which Barnett's had agreed to sell to me for £45. Although I hadn't paid them I regarded it as mine, and went ahead modifying it with a pair of BSA C11 forks and yokes and brush-painted the petrol tank bright yellow; needless to say, Ernie Smith was not amused. I eventually finished outside the time allowance, but the little Villiers-engined FB was a cracking little bike, and I later uprated it to a full 250cc with one of Vale-Onslow's conversions."

The British experts would be Bill's last outing as an official Francis Barnett works rider, but he continued to campaign his Vale Onslow 'special' in tandem with one of the newly announced C15 BSAs: a modified version that he rode as a member of the works 'number two' team in the '59 Scottish.

"Dad was an agent for BSA, so when the new C15 trials bike was announced we bought one, but I was sceptical of the energy transfer system on the works bikes, so converted mine to coil ignition and used the alternator to charge the six-volt battery for a good constant spark. This was fully justified, because by the end of Tuesday the number one team of John Draper, Brian Martin and Jeff Smith had all retired, and the following day my team-mates Tom Ellis and Arthur Lampkin had also been sidelined with similar electrical problems. I was the only one left from the BSA works teams, but, sadly, I was eliminated on the last day when the battery ran flat on the home run to the Edinburgh finish."

It was the beginning of a long association with Small Heath's unit construction singles, which would not only earn the Oxford man some good results in the important nationals like the Travers and Jefferies trials, but also his choice for two international six days. His ISDT debut in the '59 event in Wales ended on the Friday when, while still on gold medal schedule, the C15 expired. He had to wait another six years before his next six-day outing in the Isle of Man. It was described at the time as the toughest in the event's long history, and from the starting line-up of 299, only 82 – including seven British riders – survived the six, strength-sapping days, and with the exception of Bill Faulkner and his trusty B40, all of the works BSAs went out with electrical problems.

"Geoff Duke and his team had done a fantastic job squeezing an 1100-mile course out of an island which only measures 30 by 10, but they had no control over the awful weather, which made the riding conditions appalling. My B40 was the same bike I was using in one-day trials, but to make it suitable for the ISDT I'd fixed it up with lights, fitted a longer Victor rear swinging arm, a Gold Star front brake, and duplicated all of the cables. The course turned into a sea of mud, on high ground the visibility was down to a few yards, and all of us were soaking wet and exhausted from manhandling our bikes through bogs and mud holes. All of the works-entered BSA singles went out with electrical problems, but I'd spent a lot of time waterproofing mine, and amazingly the B40 kept going. By the end the rear shocks were absolutely shot, and on the final speed test around the old Clypse

Mitcham Vase trial, November 1958, on the ex-works 250cc Francis Barnett with BSA forks and Vale Onslow barrel.

On the BSA in the Clayton Cup trial, August 1961.

"ALL OF THE WORKS-ENTERED BSA SINGLES WENT OUT WITH ELECTRICAL PROBLEMS, BUT I'D SPENT A LOT OF TIME WATERPROOFING MINE, AND AMAZINGLY THE B40 KEPT GOING"

Bill looking for grip in the Tanner Trudge time trial 1962. (Courtesy Gordon Francis)

course it was like riding a pogo stick; thankfully it kept going until the end, and I came away with a bronze medal."

The following year the B40 was pensioned off and replaced by a 440 GP Victor – a gift from BSA – which, with its engine capacity stretched to 475cc, was the perfect bike to tackle the glutinous mud in the annual Tanner Trudge time trial: the super tough, strength-sapping, multi-lap event at Naish Hill in Wiltshire, in which Bill was the first to compete in both solo and sidecar classes on his BSA singles.

"I fancied having a go at sidecar trials, so as we had a 500CB BSA in the shop I fitted it with a pair of Norton forks and married it up to a chair which had once been on Arthur and Lyn Pulman's championship winning Matchless. I persuaded one of our mechanics, Roy Hancliffe, to passenger for me, and, as it's difficult to find a decent hill in Oxfordshire, we used to spend our lunch breaks practising down on the railway bank at nearby Port Meadow. Our first event was down in the Wessex centre and I was first sidecar away; somehow we got lost on our way to the first section but eventually found it and on arrival all the rest of the crews were waiting for us. No-one would go up until we had carved a rut, and, as I soon discovered, in muddy trials with a chair you didn't want to be the first man. Ron Langston was the leading sidecar man at the time, and he was just mustard: you could start in the same rut and in the same gear as Ron, but where he would

get cracking we wouldn't even get going. I really enjoyed our three seasons with the outfit; we had a lot of fun and a bit of success when we finished runner-up to Derek Rickman in the Three Musketeers. I later sold the BSA and built a Bultaco, but I couldn't get on with it, and my old pal Pat Lamper rode it with some success with his niece in the chair."

Bill would continue riding in open to centre and national trials on a variety of Spanish and Japanese two-strokes right up until the mid-'70s, and he recalls the moment he decided to call it a day.

"I'd qualified for the 1975 southern experts – run by the Frome club that year – but I'd always said that if I finished last then I would retire. On the day no-one fell by the wayside and I was last, so that was that; the end of my trials career."

It brought the curtain down on 25 fun-filled years, best summed up by the man himself.

"My three great ambitions when I started out were to get a works ride, win a national, and win an ISDT gold. I achieved the first two, and like to think I got a 'golden' bronze in the '65 six days. I was never a star, but considered myself a great enthusiast who rode for the fun of it. Looking back, perhaps my biggest downfall in trials was that I enjoyed it so much I couldn't hide my enjoyment, and always had a smile on my face."

On his booming BSAs and screaming DMW two-stroke, John was one of the West Country's leading scramblers of his generation, but, with a busy farm to run, he was denied the opportunity to take his talents to the international stage.

CHAPTER 4

JOHN TRIBLE - THE STORY OF NUMBER 30

First raced for in 1934, the three-foot high Patchquick trophy is the largest and one of the most prestigious in the scrambling world, and the list of past winners reads like a 'Who's Who' of off-road greats – famous names including Avery, Smith, Sharp, Bickers, Goss, Eastwood, and Noyce, but also that of a man who was arguably one of the best West Country scramblers of his generation: the Devon farmer John Trible. The years have seen some memorable scraps for the huge cup, but for a legion of scrambles fans the meeting at Haldon Hill in May 1960 will live forever. The setting was the steep slopes overlooking the city of Exeter, where on a hot summer Sunday the big crowd witnessed three epic races with number 30 Trible locked wheel-to-wheel with his friend but fierce rival, Paul Jarman, on their pair of booming of BSA Gold Stars. After recording one heat win apiece, the determined Trible led the final from the start, and at the end of a hard race he took the chequered flag a resounding 18 seconds ahead of the previous year's winner, Jarman. During a racing career that spanned three decades it was just one of the hundreds of wins for the popular Devonian, who with his wife, Margery, still lives just a stone's throw from the fields where he rode his first bike back in the early '50s. John takes up the story of how it all began.

"My dad was a farmer, and although he had no interest in motorcycle competition he rode a huge 1000cc Indian vee twin and sidecar outfit, which he used as his daily transport and to distribute the animal feed around the farm. I think I was about 14 when I got my first bike, a 1924 250cc Levis two-stroke which went like hell across the fields, and when I was old enough to ride on the road I passed my test on a 350cc Douglas twin. After the thrill of riding the old Levis around the farm I was keen to have a go at scrambling and with help from Colin Sanders – he ran the local garage and taught me a lot about the mechanics of motorcycles – I entered my first race. This was on Easter Monday 1953 near Newton Abbot, and I managed to finish fourth on my stripped-down ES2 road bike, which Colin transported for me in his A40 van. I raced a few more times during the summer of '53, but Colin's father was extremely religious and didn't approve of his son going to motorcycle meetings on the Sabbath. I remember once while his dad was at the chapel, Colin took me and the bike to the race meeting at Bude and then raced back home, leaving me to get a tow when the scramble was over. The ES2 was a heavy old beast, and I quickly learnt that if I was going to progress I needed something more competitive, so for the following year I ordered a new BB32 Gold Star scrambler from Bob Ray in Barnstaple. I chose the 350 simply because it meant I could race it in both the 350 and 500cc classes, and compared to the Norton the Goldie was in another league. In fact, it was so much better in one of my first races I won the Dartmouth club's Caroline Cup at Morleigh, which saw me upgraded to an expert, and by the end of the '54 season I was winning regularly in the south western centre, and even managed to beat Dave Paul, who at the time was the Cornish champion."

On leaving school, John had followed his father into farming, but had always nurtured the idea of becoming a fighter pilot. Sadly, on reaching the age for national service he was told that, as he was working on the farm, he was not required, and his quest to take to the skies would have to be put on hold for another 25 years. Despite the difficulties of balancing work and pleasure, John was beginning to spread his scrambling wings, competing at not just the Cornish and Wessex centres, but also trying his hand at some of the important trade supported nationals; although, as he recalled, in the days before the motorways, trips to far away Lancashire were long and tiring.

"For the first few seasons I'd raced mostly in my two local centres, and because at the time there was a strong adherence to the Lord's Day observance in Cornwall, most of their events were held on Saturday afternoons and evenings, which meant I could get in two meetings in the same weekend. I was always very interested in the mechanical side of things, and I loved working on and tuning the engines; this was all done in an outbuilding on the farm, and the only thing I ever farmed out was when I needed a new big end. Most of the time I was travelling with my friend and fellow racer Thornley Bailey, and although my parents were very supportive of my chosen sport, my father never saw me race, and my mum only ever came to one meeting; the speed and noise frightened her so much she never came again.

"To improve I needed to stretch myself against some of the country's best, and one of my first nationals was in the Lancs Grand National at Curedon Park. From my home in south Devon it took us all night to get to the venue, which on arrival was blanketed in thick fog. I can vividly recall the 'Le Mans' type start, where we had to run to our bikes and kickstart them into life, and the incredibly long lonely laps with just an occasional marshal to point us on our way."

John didn't figure in the results in his national debut, but he'd proven that he and his Goldie were more than capable of mixing it with the best, and it was a natural progression when he was called to represent the south west in what would be the first of his many rides in the inter-centre team scramble. Much of Trible's scrambling career would be on big four-stroke singles, but he proved equally adept on a small capacity two-stroke; on a 197cc DMW he was soon embarrassing a host of the West Country's best with his speed and sure-footed handling.

"Out of the blue I was approached by Bideford motorcycle dealer Ron Lake, who asked me if I would be interested in racing a 197cc DMW for him. In those days two-stroke tuning was very much a 'black art,' but Ron seemed to know what he was doing, and running on dope the little bike really flew. It was great, because the understanding we had was that after each meeting it was returned to Ron's shop for cleaning and preparation, and all I had to do was to race it."

In fact, John ended up racing the Lake-sponsored bike for four seasons, and during that time he recorded some impressive victories on the little two-stroke. Not only did he manage to beat Triss and Bryan

Sharp on their works Francis Barnetts at Bulbarrow Hill in Dorset, he also had a memorable day at Blindmoor where the Jarman brothers reigned supreme. Some rich pickings for the versatile Trible, who was first past the flag in the 250cc class on the little DMW, and later scooped both the two unlimited and handicap finals on the big Gold Star ahead of the similarly mounted Jarmans.

The quartet of Neil and Paul Jarman, Terry Cox and John also made up both the Somerton, Devon and Cornwall and south western team in club and inter-centre team events; numerous wins were chalked up, although, as John recalled, this didn't go down too well with all of their rivals.

"The four of us represented the south western centre for several years, and we also had the same line up for the Somerton club in the centre team championships, which we won four or five years on the trot. This led to a protest from some of the other teams, who felt that it wasn't fair we kept winning, and someone else should be given a chance. The inter-centre team races were a great opportunity to compete against the country's best, and one of my first rides came at a very muddy Brill where in some horrendous conditions – in which most of us were struggling to keep moving – Ron Langston made it look all too easy on his works Ariel, and won both legs convincingly. Undoubtedly our best result as a team came at Shrubland Park, where we all had great rides, and finished runner-up to the very strong Midland line-up led by Jeff Smith. Jeff was a master in almost any conditions, and one of my best performances against him came when I was picked by Geoff Ward to represent the south in the annual race against the north. When the gate dropped I had a super start, and held second spot behind Gordon Blakeway with Smithy breathing down my neck in third. I managed to hold him off for five laps, but he eventually slipped past to win from Gordon, with me – feeling very chuffed – in fourth."

Living and working on the family farm in the far south west meant that, despite plenty of offers to ride on the continent, John's racing was restricted to the UK. However, his talent was there for all to see, and in early 1958 he secured his first works ride.

"From competing and doing reasonably well in the trade-supported nationals I'd got a few chains and tyres, but other than the DMW supplied by Ron Lake all of my bikes were those I bought and ran myself. In an effort to try and drum up some support Ron and I went to all of the main factories, and on the back of this, BSA – who by now had phased out the smaller Goldie – agreed to make me a DB350 to go with the secondhand 500 I bought from the dealer Alan Brotherton, and shortly afterwards Royal Enfield offered me a works 500 for the 1958 season. The agreement was that they would supply me with a free bike – as ridden by Don and Derek Rickman in '57 – plus any spares, but it would be up to me to keep it fettled, and there would be no pay involved. In the engine compartment – top speed wise – the Enfield was on a par with the Gold Star, but, as I quickly discovered, when pushed hard the frame broke, and the gearbox was decidedly dodgy; the same problems that Derek and Don had encountered the previous year. When the gearbox failed another cluster would soon be sent from Redditch, but they were exactly the same as the old ones and nothing was ever done to improve things. The Rickmans had improved the handling by fitting BSA forks, but I was continually frustrated by breakdowns, often when I was in the lead, and at the end of the second season I returned the bike to Enfields and continued as a privateer on my pair of new Gold Stars."

John already showing the style that would make him one of the best in the south west.

"ON A 197cc DMW HE WAS SOON EMBARRASSING A HOST OF THE WEST COUNTRY'S BEST WITH HIS SPEED AND SURE-FOOTED HANDLING"

John flying on the works Royal Enfield.

Leading at the start of an unlimited race in 1960 – just look at the crowd!

Back on the old faithful BSAs, John was soon back to his winning ways, although he was out of luck when he rode in one of the first televised scrambles. Organised by the ex-Ariel works rider Bob Ray at Fremington near Barnstaple, it quickly turned into a mudbath; similar conditions to those John encountered at Pirbright later the same season.

"I had my two new Goldies for the 1960 season, and although I didn't figure in the results at the TV scramble, I notched up some good wins, including the Patchquick trophy, and had a good ride at Draper's farm, but sadly I had to miss the big race at Hawkstone Park because it was harvest time and I couldn't get away from the farm. Scrambling might have been a 'summer sport,' but we raced in some pretty appalling conditions and some of the worst were in that year's Sunbeam point-to-point at East Meon. After days of heavy rain the mud was horrendous, and in the 350cc race I managed to get up to second, but it was all I could do to keep moving. and eventually the front wheel got so clogged it wouldn't go round and I had to get off and push up the steep hill to the finish."

Despite having no trials experience – he only ever rode in one event in Cornwall on a 350cc AJS – John was a master in the mud, and

his neat and tidy riding style ensured that crashes and injuries were few and far between. However the tumbles were inevitable, and his worst injury came at the most inopportune time: the week before his wedding.

"Margery used to come and support me all across the country, and the weekend before our wedding I was racing at a meeting at Ladcock, near Truro. I was flying on the Goldie, but on entering a wood I got my toe caught on a stump resulting in a broken foot, which meant that I had to go to our wedding on crutches; as you can imagine, I wasn't very popular! Up until then the only other nasty injury I'd sustained was at Higher Farm Wick near Glastonbury, where after getting a cracking start I led into the first corner, but Joe Johnson knocked me off. I landed heavily and was carried off to the medical tent with concussion."

The late '50s and early '60s was a golden era for scrambling, with huge crowds at the West Country meetings, many cheering on local star Trible on his big BSAs.

"Because I was into bikes I was always treated as bit of an outcast by my mother's family – auctioneers and heavily into horses – but I had terrific support from the local press and the fans across Devon.

John on his way to second at the Somerset GN scramble at Little Norton, 1959. (Courtesy Gordon Francis)

A super all-action shot on the Goldie in 1963.

The late '60s, but still a force to be reckoned with on the B50.

One of the Holsworthy coach companies used to organise a bus to all of the West Country events I rode in, and even the police were keen to know how I'd got on. I remember once on returning from a meeting in Cornwall, I was knocking on a bit with my car and trailer when they pulled me over. I thought they were going to book me for speeding, but they just wanted to know who'd won, and when I told them it was me they smiled, said 'Well done,' and told me to watch my speed on the way home. I raced all across the country, but among my favourite meetings were those held during the summer on Wednesday evenings at Exmouth in east Devon. Because of the exposure scrambling was getting on the TV with the winter *Grandstand* and *World Of Sport* series, the Exmouth events – held on a great course overlooking the sea – always attracted some huge holiday crowds, and also some of the big boys like Jeff Smith and his works BSA team-mates. The racing was always fierce and very competitive, but there was a great sense of camaraderie, and if there was a problem we all helped each other out. I remember at one of the meetings my front wheel collapsed after the Goldie had landed from a particularly big jump on the rock hard ground. I thought that there would be no more racing for me that evening, but just as I was about to load up, Smithy brought along his spare for me to use. A great piece of sportsmanship, and typical of what went on in the pits in those days."

For his many fans, it was a sad day when John announced his retirement at the end of the 1961 season, but the lure of scrambling was a strong one, and four years later he was back in the saddle again – unsurprisingly, on another of his much loved 500cc Gold Stars.

"Because of pressure of work on the farm and a young family, I decided that at the end of the '61 season it was time to call it a day, and sold my Goldie for £115. I'd packed it up for four or five years and was then approached by a friend in the village who'd just bought a Gold Star scrambler, and he asked me if I would like to race it for him. After talking it over with Margery I decided to give it a go, although, from the outset, I made my mind up it was going to be purely for fun. I wasn't going to be racing every week, and my outings would be limited purely to the Cornish and south western centre. By then the big Gold Star had lost its competitive edge against the Metisse and big bore two-strokes, and after two seasons my friend part-exchanged for a unit construction 441. This was later bored out to a full 500cc, and when housed in one of Tony Burgess' works replica frames it handled like a dream, and was a lovely bike to ride. I managed to chalk up a few wins, but the only times I rode it out of the West Country was when I represented the south west in the annual inter-centre team races. I continued to ride the Victor up until the end of the 1976 season, but by then I was past my best, and decided it was time to hang my leathers up for good."

It finally brought the curtain down on the scrambling career of John Trible: the popular farmer from Devon, who was one of the unsung heroes from a golden era in motorcycle sport.

When John won the Patchquick in 1960, he took home the trophy in his Bedford van, next to the Gold Star. Today, because of its value, it is kept in a bank vault and brought out only for the annual race. In 1978 he achieved his boyhood dream when he got his pilot's licence, and for three memorable seasons – 2004/2006 – he was the 'bouncer' in his old friend Gordon Jackson's trials car. Big thanks to John and Margery for their time and hospitality, and for some wonderful memories from those halcyon days.

Fancy headgear for Olga on the 125cc James in 1950.

A woman who lived life to the full, Olga was one of the leading female riders of her generation. A true all-rounder, she not only rode in one- and six-day trials, but also turned her talents to scrambles and road racing – the latter on both two and four wheels – and was more than capable of showing the male opposition a clean pair of heels.

CHAPTER 5

OLGA KEVELOS – PRECIOUS MEMORIES

With a 22-year riding career that encompassed the strength-sapping international six days, one-day observation trials, scrambles, road racing and formula three racing cars, Olga Kevelos was undoubtedly one of the sports greatest ever female competitors. She may have been born into an era where females were generally viewed as the gentler sex, but this lady proved herself to be no shrinking violet. Shortly before she died in November 2009 I was lucky enough to talk to her about those golden years, when the girl in the leather flying helmet took on, and often beat, the cream of the largely male-dominated competition world.

Olga was the child of a Greek father and English mother, who raised her as the typical English young lady in the refined area of Edgbaston in Birmingham. She told me a little of those early years.

"My father had no interest in motorcycling, but he loved car racing, and I remember vividly the day he took me to Donnington Park to watch the 1939 Grand Prix. As it transpired it would be the last held there before the outbreak of the Second World War, but it was a fantastic meeting, and the sight of Nuvolari wrestling his huge car around the Donnington curves lives with me to this day.

"After I left King Edward's School I started work with the Greenwich Royal Observatory, and on the outbreak of war moved with them to Bath. I was there for a while, but when the call for mobilisation came I applied for a job as a trainee inland waterways boatwoman. I was taken on, and for the next two years was part of a three-girl crew manning a pair of barges carrying sheet metal and ingots from London to Birmingham on the Grand Union canal and then on to Coventry, to pick up coal for the return trip to London. Living conditions were rough to say the least, and most days we would be working for 18 to 20 hours with little or no respite."

Those two hard years on the canal boats prepared Olga both mentally and physically for her later exploits in the international six-day trials, as did her postwar travels around Europe and the near and far east.

"At the end of the war a friend and I obtained government grants to study for a year at a university in Paris, and I then travelled around Europe and Asia for a while before returning home to decide on my future. My father worked in the stock exchange but he'd bought a restaurant – the Cherry Orchard in central Birmingham – and it was agreed that as my two brothers and I were looking for something to do we would take it over. By then I'd had my first ride on a motorcycle –

an Ariel Square Four sidecar outfit belonging to an artist friend – and although I didn't have a licence he let me take it for a spin on the road. I discovered I had a natural flair, and decided it was time to get a bike of my own. Birmingham, of course, was very much the centre of the British motorcycle industry, and many of our clientele in the restaurant were names in the trade. One of them was Phil Heath – at the time almost a habitué in the Cherry Orchard – and after he took me to watch my first race meeting at Cadwell Park I was hooked and bought an ex-WD Royal Enfield from him. Charlie Markham – the Midland editor of *Motor Cycling* – was also a regular in the restaurant, and in January 1948 he invited me along to the inaugural meeting of the Solihull motorcycle club, where he introduced me to Arthur Kimberley. Arthur was the managing director of James Motorcycles, and he told me all about their prewar factory ladies' trials team, and how the sport was now much the poorer for their absence. Before the evening was out he asked me if I would like to ride a James in the Scottish Six Days trial, to which I replied 'Yes, please.' I didn't have a clue what a trial was, but thought that it sounded a lot of fun, and I entered a Birmingham 30 club event. The bike Arthur supplied me with was a 125 based on the wartime ML model and I had a pretty good ride; in fact much to everyone's surprise – my own included – when the results arrived I discovered I'd won an award. On the strength of this James offered me a works bike for the Scottish, so to prepare myself for the big event I entered the Travers trial, which entailed riding the bike all the way from Birmingham to the north of England and back again after the event."

It was hard work, but it gave the young Olga an insight into what competition motorcycling was all about, and a few weeks later she was off to Fort William – this time on the train – with the regular James team comprising the three Normans, Palmer, Moore, and Hooton.

"It was a tough event, and it felt like I had to carry the bike as much as I rode it. The little two-stroke would only go for about 20 miles, and then I had to get the tools out and change the sparkplug. The crowds were great and gave me lots of encouragement, but the James eventually cried 'enough' on the last day when the magneto died, and I had to retire."

It would be the first of 18 rides in the Scottish for Olga, who by September 1948 was on her way to Italy for her first international six-day trial on a new 350cc AJS.

"Hugh Viney was winning most of the major trials on his 350cc AJS, so when my entry for that year's international six-day trial was accepted I bought myself a similar 350 single. Most of the British riders either transported their bikes to the San Remo start by car and trailer or on the train but I decided to ride there. My lone journey across France was quite an adventure in itself, as the roads were still very badly potholed from the war, I had difficulty finding my way, and then 'lost' a day after I had slightly too much to drink in an overnight B&B and had to sleep it off."

Cruising through Ventimiglia with her distinctive cyclamen-coloured headscarf flowing in the wind, Olga was spotted by journalist Cyril Quantrill, who headed her off with the news that she was late for the weigh-in and there was no time for sightseeing. She made it to San Remo and got the bike through scrutineering, but there was no time for last minute fettling before the AJS was locked away in the parc ferme for the night. The event would go down in ISDT history as 'the Grand Prix of the goat tracks,' and as the riders got under way on day one the

biggest cheer was reserved for Olga: the event's lone lady competitor. The route took the riders along tortuous unguarded mountain tracks, but, despite suffering an early tumble, Olga completed day one on time. Sadly, her hopes of gold were dashed on day two when she had a head-on collision with a car on a narrow track, finishing the day in hospital. The pain of her broken bones was eased by generous supplies of local vino, but when it was time to leave there was the small matter of the hospital bill to be settled.

"I was well looked after by the nuns in the hospital, but they wouldn't let me leave until I'd paid the bill for my treatment and the bottles of wine. Immediately postwar we were only allowed to take £25 out of the UK, and I had little money left, but when Major Nicholls from BAOR came to collect me I discovered everything had been cleared for me to leave. At the time I didn't know how or why, but sometime later I leaned from Helen Chamberlain that her husband, Peter – the British team manager – had won some money at the casino, and it was he who paid the hospital bill."

There was an even bigger surprise in store for Olga at the prize-giving, when, after the winning British Trophy and Vase teams collected their silverware, she was presented with one of three very special awards for outstanding gallant performances.

During the winter of 1948/49 the AJS brought Olga considerable success in both the national trade-supported trials and also the Scottish Six Days, but, by the time September's ISDT came around, she was mounted on a 500T Norton.

"With the British team's victory in Italy the previous year, Wales was chosen for the 1949 ISDT, which meant it was only a short ride from my home in Birmingham to the trials headquarters in Llandrindod Wells. The 500T was one of the first pukka trials bikes on the market, and after seeing one in Frank Cope's Hagley Road showroom I decided it was the perfect bike for both one- and six-day events. To prepare myself for the international I did a few open to centre scrambles during the summer of '49, and by the time September came around I'd been upgraded to an expert and was feeling fit and pretty confident with the bike."

Olga's optimism was well-founded, as the Norton ran faultlessly, and after a spirited ride the event's lone female competitor returned to her Birmingham home with a coveted gold medal for her efforts.

"Both locally and nationally my gold medal generated a lot of publicity. Frank Cope put the bike on display in his showroom and generously knocked £5 off my HP repayments. The Norton factory was delighted, and rebuilt it for me with many special parts in the engine, and they also invited me along to their stand at the motorcycle show where I was presented to Princess Margaret."

Before the 1950 ISDT came around – again based in Llandrindod Wells – Olga had another winter of one-day trials, the Scottish, and a season of scrambles under her belt, the highlight of which was finishing runner-up to BSA works rider Brian Martin in that year's Grand National.

"Trials were my first love, but scrambles were a lot of fun, and throughout the '50s I raced all sorts of bikes. The 500T was a real jack-of-all-trades machine, and was very competitive in the standard tyre class races that many of the clubs used to run. All of us who rode in the '49 international were asked by clerk of the course Harry Baughan what improvements we would like to see for the 1950, event to which I replied 'Some ladies' loos at the lunch stops.'"

Off-Road Giants!

These were duly supplied, but they remained little used as, out of the four lady riders, Pat Hughes and Jill Savage retired on the first day, and Olga's Norton blew up on day three, leaving Mollie Briggs to enjoy the 'lady competitors only' marquee on her own.

At the end of the season, Norton reduced its trials support, and Olga joined Mollie Briggs and Anne Newton in the James ladies trials team, but, as she recalled, the girls didn't think too much of their new claret and blue riding colours.

"Arthur Kimberley had us decked out in the Aston Villa football colours, and the only way we could deaden them down was to stop and smear mud onto our light blue woolly hats."

1951 was a busy year for the Birmingham girl, as, in addition to trials and scrambles, she'd begun short circuit racing on Ernie Earles' International Norton, and also sampled a Manx-engined Keift single-seater racing car. With two and four wheels she was a natural, and in an early outing in the Keift at Brands Hatch, she was leading until the last lap, when, after receiving an instruction from the pits to slow down, she was pipped at the post. "Shame," she said, "because at the time I could have done with the £15 first prize money."

A 125cc Parilla was her choice of machine for the 1951 international in Varese, but hopes of another gold medal were dashed on day five, when a crash left Olga with little to smile about.

"Prior to the trial I asked Signor Parilla if I could spend some time at the factory familiarising myself with the machine, but he said 'Don't worry, the mechanics will do it all.' The first morning's ride went well enough, but after the lunch break the officials tried to restart us in the same order as we started, instead of our correct time schedules. When they refused to give out the time cards, pandemonium broke out in the parc ferme, and, confronted by 250 very unhappy competitors, the officials locked themselves into a wooden shed, which was attacked by the mob and quickly reduced to matchwood. Along the route there were quite a few of the home nation's bikes being worked on illegally, and before the Wednesday night run I was also 'hijacked' near to the Lake Como checkpoint, where the Parilla was wheeled away into a garage and its magneto was changed by the works mechanics. It was a great little bike, and I was on gold medal schedule for the first four days, but on the fifth I overdid things on a tricky downhill section and the bike went over a cliff. The Parilla was wrecked, and I was left with two missing front teeth and lots of bruises; the headline in *La Stampa* read (in Italian) 'Olga lost her smile,' but Signor Parilla was so pleased with all the publicity he paid me a bonus, and also gave me a gold watch to make up for the gold medal I almost won."

After winning a bronze in a super tough event in Austria in 1952, Olga was invited to ride a Czechoslovakian two-stroke for the '53 international, but her acceptance brought the wrath of the manufacturer's union boss, Major Watling.

"Major Watling said it was bad enough that I should ride a foreign bike again, but one from a communist country was 'beyond the pale.' The CZ/Jawa factory invited me to Prague six weeks before the trial, but any thoughts I might have had about having a nice holiday lasted about three days. After a quick tour of Prague, I was off to Gottwaldov in the Tatra mountains, where I was put under the charge of a lovely English-speaking man named Doctor Schulman, who gave me the nickname of 'Kelevlosova.' At the mountain retreat I joined the 60 or so Czech riders entered for the international, and I soon discovered it was going to be a tough six weeks. Typically our day started at 6am

Furious footing on the little CZ in the 1955 Scottish Six Days.

with breakfast followed by tough physical training, and then a ride of 200 miles or so across ISDT type terrain. On return to base we had maintenance lessons and more practice, before turning in at 10pm; I can't remember how many times I stripped and rebuilt the engine of my CZ, but by the end of the six weeks I could do it almost blindfolded, and with all the physical training, I'd never felt fitter in my life."

In the event itself the super fit Olga had a brilliant ride on the Czech two-stroke, and at the end of six hard days returned to England with her second gold medal, but minus her other prizes and presents.

"Prior to going to Czechoslovakia, some friends there had asked me to take as many pairs of MkVII goggles as I could, and after a quick trip around Birmingham I managed to buy 30 pairs, which cost me about £30. Quality goggles were unavailable behind the Iron Curtain, and the Czechs were delighted with them, so with the money they gave me I had enough to pay for excess baggage on the flight back home. However, when I arrived at the airport I was told that excess baggage could be only paid for in sterling or dollars, and with the argument getting more and more heated I just dumped all my presents – mostly glassware – and prizes on the floor and stormed through the boarding

Negotiating a watersplash at the Colmore Cup trial in 1951.

"CONFRONTED BY 250 VERY UNHAPPY COMPETITORS, THE OFFICIALS LOCKED THEMSELVES INTO A WOODEN SHED, WHICH WAS ATTACKED BY THE MOB AND QUICKLY REDUCED TO MATCHWOOD"

Trying out an early Greeves – Bert Greeves decided to disregard Olga's suggestions on how to improve it.

On Len Vale Onslow's 197cc Valon in 1960 – a clean ride here, but Olga retired later with mechanical problems.

With Pat and Les Wise and the Ariel Arrow at Thruxton in 1962.

gate shouting that it was totally ridiculous, and on return to England I would be writing a letter to *The Times*. I cooled down on the flight home and said goodbye to the glassware, but three weeks later an enormous crate arrived at my home containing everything I had left on the airport floor, all carefully packed with nothing damaged. A couple of months later two more huge crates turned up at the door, but this time they contained two lightweight trials bikes. After the ISDT the CZ director had asked me to have the bike and ride it in one-day trials, but when I told them it was unsuitable they invited me to draft out a rough design of what I required. The two bikes duly turned up, and I rode the twin port Jawa version in the Scottish Six Days, but although it was well made and handled okay, the engine power characteristics were all wrong, and it was a bit of a struggle on some of the nadgery stuff."

The one-day Jawa trials iron required work to make it competitive, but the tie-up with the Czech factory led to other

memorable trips behind the Iron Curtain, and Olga told me about a three-day trial in Poland – and also a scramble in Russia – that drew a vast crowd; an event memorable for numerous crashes and lots of bruised bodies.

"The Polish WSK factory invited me to ride one of their bikes – a Bantam lookalike copied from the same DKW – in the 1954 Tatra three-day trial, which I flew to with the AMC pair of Bob Manns and Gordon Jackson. It was held in high temperatures, and extremely tough, like a mini 'international' featuring both observed sections and timed enduro-style runs, and really hard work on a low-powered 125cc two-stroke! The Russian scramble was on the shores of the Black Sea, and very much like an open to centre event back home, but it attracted a huge crowd of around 70,000, who arrived jam-packed into old buses and trucks. Most of the riders were on Urals, which were a bit rough and not ideally suited to scrambling, and there were lots of crashes. There were many bruised and bloodied bodies, but there was scant concern from the Russian manager, Boris Tramm, who said to me 'Don't worry about the riders, they are expendable and we've got plenty more.'"

Olga loved the formula three racing, but by the end of her second season she'd become disenchanted with the Keift, and moved on to a sweeter-handling car made by Rex McCandless.

"The 1100cc JAP-engined Keift had a lot of poke and was fine on bends, but the steering – operated by a conventional car steering wheel – left a lot to be desired. It was difficult to keep on the road in a straight line, and it seemed like you needed three hands to drive it. Over in Ireland Rex McCandless had designed and built his own version of a formula three racer, on which he'd incorporated a motorcycle handlebar and controls in place of the car steering wheel, and it was a revelation compared to what I'd driven before."

Olga had a busy season racing the McCandless car in Ireland,

Olga on the 250cc James in the Clayton trial in 1963.

and admitted it made a 'nice change from the bikes,' but two wheels were her passion, and throughout the 1950s there was barely a top class event where the name of Kevelos didn't appear in the results. During that decade she also rode many different machines, including an early Greeves, an ex-works BSA Bantam, and an unusual 250cc Valon that she took to the Highlands for the '58 Scottish Six Days.

"In 1954 Bert Greeves had just started making his first competition machines, and he lent me one on the understanding that after a couple of months I submitted a report on his new bike. I rode it in the Red Rose national and a couple of local events and sent him my findings, which suggested that 'the model had promise but needed modifications.' However, this didn't go down too well with Mr Greeves, who had great pride in his creations, and he sent me a brief note in reply which read 'Please return it on the next train to Thundersly.' That was the end of my 'works' Greeves, but interestingly much of what I suggested was later implemented by Brian Stonebridge when he joined them in 1957. I replaced the Greeves with yet another James, and the following year I found myself on an ex-John Draper 150cc BSA Bantam. The Bantam was a bit delicate but a super little bike, and I had some good rides on it, including the '57 Scottish and several other important nationals that season. I was always interested in trying out different machinery, and for the '58 event I manage to cadge a 250cc Valon from Len Vale Onslow. This was made by Len in his workshop in Birmingham, and featured BSA Bantam wheels, C11 forks, and was powered by one of his specially converted 32A Villiers engines. It was a well-thought-out machine, but the fact I made it to the Fort William start line was a miracle, as we didn't finish putting it together until 3am of the morning I was due to set off for Scotland. Considering there was no time to test the bike I had a pretty good ride, but on arrival at one section I was asked by the following rider why my back wheel was running about six inches out of line with the front. Closer examination revealed that the frame had fractured, and was gradually coming apart beneath me."

As the '60s dawned Olga continued to compete in both one-day and the Scottish six-day trials, but, as she told me, lady riders were not met with open arms by some scramble clubs.

"Ladies were not always welcome or even allowed by the organisers of some important scrambles, although the SUNBAC club was a notable exception. On the road race circuits BEMSEE was always kindly disposed to us, and looking back I think my biggest regret is that I didn't do more tarmac racing."

One of Olga's last road races was the 1962 Thruxton 500 miler, which ended in retirement when the 250cc Ariel arrow she was sharing with Pat Wise seized at the 100-mile mark, but she continued to compete in both one-day trials and the ISDTs, which in 1964 took her to East Germany.

"Riding in the ISDTs behind the Iron Curtain gave me a real insight as to what it was like for the people living there, and I was aware that our every move was closely scrutinised, especially those of the American team, which included their Hollywood star, Steve McQueen. We were told that the breakfasts – which consisted mainly of cold boiled eggs and raw salads – were 'designed by doctors,' but they were certainly like nothing we were used to at home. We had plenty of fruit – I later discovered all the food had been especially brought in for the event – and in the parc ferme I offered some to the inquisitive local children. They were extremely puzzled by the bananas, as they had never seen them before and had no idea how to peel them, but before I could show them the police pounced shouting 'forbidden, forbidden,' and ushered the children away.

"Waiting for the trial to start there was little to do, so after the Saturday weigh-in a group of us went by minibus to visit the former concentration camp at nearby Belsen. This was a harrowing experience which left me very de-tuned for the trial, in which I was forced to retire when I ran out of time on my 50cc Honda."

Although the little Honda didn't have the legs to make it a serious six days trial bike, the single cylinder four-stroke and its 90cc sibling were willing and ultra-reliable workhorses, as Olga discovered over seven long, hard days and nights at Goodwood in 1964.

"I was part of the team of riders brought in by Honda for their attempt at the Maudes trophy, which meant we had to keep the little 90cc step-throughs running continuously for seven days and nights around the Goodwood race circuit. Our schedule saw us two hours on and four hours off riding the bikes, but during our time off we were also expected to take turns driving the cars containing the ACU officials who were scrutinising the run. As you can imagine, riding a low speed bike round and round a race circuit for seven days was incredibly boring, but unlike the Ford Cortinas, which developed all sorts of suspension problems, the Honda singles never missed a beat, and we were later awarded the Maudes trophy for our efforts."

Throughout the 1960s Olga continued to compete in all of the major nationals and the Scottish Six Days on a Dot, a James, and later a 250cc Butler, but as her own riding began to taper off she became increasingly involved with organising events for the Birmingham club. These included the 1967 British experts, in which, as clerk of the course, she controversially disqualified virtually the whole entry for hanging about at sections. The only rider to escape was the Ulsterman John Harrison, who had to get round quickly as he had to catch an evening boat back home to Belfast, and, as a result, he was unexpectedly crowned winner of the '67 British experts.

Olga brought the curtain down on her competitive motorcycling career with the international six-day trial in Spain in 1970, and with it came the end of a golden era. Twenty-two fantastic years, in which the young woman from Birmingham won the love and respect of the crowds and her fellow competitors with her skill and never-say-die attitude.

Olga Kevelos, 1923-2009

A very muddy Gothington Gallop in 1949. (Courtesy Bill Cole)

Not only a top class scrambler, but a clever and innovative engineer, who, back in the 1950s, won hundreds of races on some interesting specials that were fabricated in the shed at the bottom of his garden.

CHAPTER 6

TOMMY BARKER – SCRAMBLING STAR

During his glittering 15-year scrambles career between 1948 and the end of '62, there were few events in the western and Wessex centres in which the name of Tommy Barker and his home-brewed specials didn't feature in the results. Over 50 years have now slipped by since Tommy hung up his helmet and racing leathers, but, as I discovered on a trip to south Gloucestershire, his memories of those golden days and the epic battles with the likes of Bill Nicholson, Brian Stonebridge, and the Rickman and Sharp brothers are still crystal clear. He began by telling me how in the austere postwar years he began his scrambles career on a 500cc BSA, and about the little TBS: the bike on which, in 1949, he beat the BSA works star Nicholson to win the prestigious Cotswold Cup.

"I was born in Wrotham, Kent, in May 1926, but my family moved to Dursley in the depressed 1930s when my father found work as a carpenter, and it was there I began my working career with a job at Listers, in 1941. Three years later I had my call-up papers for the army, and was enlisted into the Royal Engineers for a posting to India to learn how to service fridges and air-conditioning units. After a while I was transferred to Iraq, near Basra, and it was here I got my first taste of off-road riding. I was issued with a G3L Matchless, which was my

transport to the various army units to service their refrigerators, but it was like a civvy job, as I only had to work in the mornings, and as there was plenty of petrol about, in the afternoons a gang of us used to go off into the desert, riding over the rough stuff on our bikes. It was great fun, and I made up my mind that when my army time was up I was going to start riding in trials and scrambles. Every week I used to send a postal order to my mum to save for me until I got back home, and on my return in 1948 I had enough to buy a brand new B34 BSA.

"My first event was a Dursley club trial, but I was drawn to the speed of scrambling, and in the summer of '48 I raced the BSA in a couple of events – at Maysmoor and Turley in the Gloucester GN – for bikes with standard tyres. The following year I part-exchanged the B34 for a 350cc Goldie, which, before the days when I could afford a car or van, was transported to events all around the western centre on a flatbed side-valve BSA sidecar outfit with my girlfriend – later my wife – Doreen riding pillion. In the early '30s the then chancellor, Phil Snowden, had introduced a half-price road tax for motorcycles under 150cc, so when scrambling started again after the war quite a lot of clubs introduced races for these lightweights. In early '49 my brother alerted me to a non-running 150cc BSA that was for sale on a farm in

An early shot of Tommy on the rigid-framed 350cc BSA at Worcester in the late 1940s. (Courtesy Bill Cole)

Yorkshire, so, egged on by fellow club members, I sent the owner £5, and a few days later the bike arrived at Dursley station. We soon got it running, and before its first race at the Cotswold I replaced the road mudguards with alloy ones, and converted it from hand to foot change. In the race I stalled it on the start line and got away last, but the little BSA was a real flyer, and by the time we got round on the first lap I'd overtaken the entire field, including Bill Nicholson on his works Bantam, and ran out a clear winner. For the 1950 season the western centre decided to downsize the engine capacity in the lightweight class to 125cc, so, using Phil Irving's book *Tuning For Speed* as reference, I spent a lot of hours during the winter of 49/50 working on the engine and improving the running gear. Running on methanol, the engine was very quick for a 125, and I married this up to a lightweight Albion four-speed gearbox and changed the girder forks for a set from a Bantam, which I filled with rubber to improve their damping. So it didn't get confused with a Bantam I called it the TBS and other than a meeting at Kidston when it went bang when the crank pin broke it was both fast and extremely reliable."

During the course of the next three or four seasons Barker and the TBS – which by now had a spring frame – notched up numerous wins,

and the records show that in 1953 alone he recorded 76 race victories on the little four-stroke. Although he loved racing his 125cc special, he was still having a lot of success on the big 'Beezer,' and, as he recalled, there were also a couple of outings on a brace of factory Dots.

"To improve the handling of the 350cc BSA I had it fitted with a McCandless swinging arm, but I had lots of problems with the rear spindle bending. On closer examination I discovered that the swinging arm pivot had been positioned out of line, and it was also too low, which meant that the chain was too tight when landing from a jump. At the time I was working for Williams and Thomas' bike shop in Stroud, and after examining all different sorts of machines I decided that the only one to have the swinging arm perfectly positioned was that of a Velocette. Using this as a guideline I went ahead and fabricated one of my own out of some tubing I bent to shape, and with a cable-operated rear wheel from an M model BSA it worked a treat. For the first two or three seasons most of my racing was in my home western and nearby Wessex centres, but, by the early '50s, I started to spread my wings to include national events like the Lancs GN and Hawkstone Park for the big 'Coronation' scramble. I remember this meeting was extremely dusty, and I needed some extra air filtering for the big BSA, so I asked if

1950 Cotswold: Tom on the 125 TBS leads Bill Nicholson on his works Bantam – Tom first, Bill second. (Courtesy Bill Cole)

"BY THE TIME WE GOT ROUND ON THE FIRST LAP I'D OVERTAKEN THE ENTIRE FIELD, INCLUDING BILL NICHOLSON ON HIS WORKS BANTAM, AND RAN OUT A CLEAR WINNER"

Aviating the BSA at Hawkstone Park in 1953. (Courtesy Bill Cole)

The TBS flying at Maisemore in July 1954. (Courtesy Bill Cole)

they could put out over the public address if there was a lady who could let me have a stocking. They were pretty hard to get and expensive in those days, but I got 34 and made the sports page of one of the national newspapers!

"On my TBS I'd had some great scraps with the factory Dots ridden by Bill Baraugh and Terry Cheshire, and with Terry away on army duties the same year – 1953 – I got the offer to ride a pair of factory-prepared bikes at some selected meetings. I had a 125 and 197 for the Worcester Traders scramble, and they went quite well, but in the Gloucester Grand National my bike stopped, and, despite my best efforts, it steadfastly refused to restart, so I left it propped against the railings and walked back to the pits. I don't think that was appreciated by Dots, but a few weeks later I had another outing on the 197 at the notorious Lancashire Grand National at Holcombe Moor. On race day it was pouring with rain, and I had to borrow Maureen's mac for a bit of extra protection. It was a Le Mans-type start, and at the sound of the siren we had to run to our bikes, fire them up, and set off on the long

three-mile lap. Sadly, with the heavy rain the track turned into a sea of liquid peat, which was like riding in glue, and although I managed to get round, the factory two-stroke was absolutely gutless, and by the finish Maureen's mac was ripped to shreds; needless to say it was my last ride on the works Dot."

His silky smooth riding style meant that a Barker crash was a rarity, but a nasty spill on the big BSA at the '55 Cotswold resulted in a broken collar bone, which sidelined him for several months. However, the time spent away from the racetracks was extremely productive, as, on his return, the BSA had been sold, and in its place was another home-made special. Powered by a 250cc Velocette, the little four-stroke single soon proved its mettle, and over the course of the next five seasons it carried the Gloucester-based man to scores of victories. Tommy takes up the story of how the bike came about, and also recalled a couple of his best rides in '58.

"I had seen Les Archer go well on his 250cc Velo, so I knew that the engine had potential, and when one came up for sale in the nearby

First season on the very tidy 250cc Velocette in 1957. (Courtesy Bill Cole)

"HIS SILKY SMOOTH
RIDING STYLE MEANT
THAT A BARKER
CRASH WAS A
RARITY"

On the 250cc Velocette at Howle Hill in 1960.
(Courtesy Bill Cole)

village of Eastcombe I decided to buy it. To try to get the best out of the engine, my boss, Ernie Thomas – a prewar continental circus road racer – had a word with Charles Udall at Velocette, who suggested that we use Venom cams which would give the same timing as a KTT. I changed the clutch for a multiplate one from an MAC along with a gearbox from a 500 MSS, and built this into a spring frame I made from scratch, using a crashed BSA B33 swinging arm and rear hub with a set of forks and hub from a B31 on the front. It was no lightweight, but it handled a treat, and once it was wound up it was very fast for a 250."

The '58 season had started well for Barker, with a win over the two-strokes of Alan Bell and Ken Messenger at the Bristol club's Henley scramble at Yatton: a victory that gave him plenty of confidence for the following weekend's encounter with some of the country's best 250 riders at the national Wessex event at Glastonbury.

"It was the first time since 1950 that the organising Tor club had got full national status for this historic event, and, keen to attract top riders like Brian Stonebridge and the Sharp and Rickman brothers, they offered a £20 purse for the winner in each class. On the day a crowd of over 10,000 lined the 1.3-mile course, which, thanks to a period of dry weather, was in perfect condition for some fast and close racing. At that time I was able to use the Velocette in both the 250 and larger capacity races, so it was good to get a feel for the track before the big race. In the first race for 350s I had a decent ride to finish fourth behind Andy Lee, Phil Nex, and Roy Bradley, and was feeling pretty confident when we came to the line for the six-lap Wessex lightweight race. Brian Stonebridge had brought along his works Greeves, which he'd fitted with one of the Herman Meier exhaust systems, and from the drop of the flag he shot into the lead followed by myself, with Triss and Bryan Sharp in hot pursuit. Brian led for the whole race, with Triss and Bryan pushing me on the 'twiddly' bits, but the Velo was quick enough to leave them on the steep hill which led into a field where they would catch me again. As we went into the last lap Stonebridge was still in the lead, but, as I flew along the long top straight, I was aware of a bit of a commotion on the side of the track with a rider obviously having trouble with his bike. Not that I had much time to look around, and as I came down the hill, round the hayrick, and up to and past the chequered flag the crowd was going wild. I thought that it was a lot of fuss for finishing second, but then Doreen told me 'You've won.' It transpired Stonebridge's Greeves had nipped up on the last lap, and although he got it fired up again he had to be content with third. With the £6 I'd already won in the 350 race, I went home with £26 prize money in my pocket, and felt like a millionaire."

After his stunning win at Glastonbury, Tommy was approached by Mr Bourne – the top man at the ACU – to ride in that year's British round of the 250cc Coupe D'Europe at Beenham Park, where, on a blisteringly hot day, he lined up against the best riders in the world. Two strength-sapping races of 45 minutes-plus per lap proved very different to his usual four- or six-lap sprint, but the 32-year-old from Gloucester certainly gave a good account of himself. At the end of a long, hard day – in which he recorded two top ten finishes – Barker and his home-brewed Velocette were eighth overall: a fantastic achievement for both the rider and the bike that he'd conceived, built, prepared, and tuned himself. The race at Beenham in 1958 turned out to be Tommy's one and only appearance on the world stage, but there would be plenty more wins – and two more Velocettes – before he eventually retired from scrambling at the end of the '62 season. He takes up the story again.

"Because I was racing the 250cc Velo in every class it was taking quite a hammering, so in 1959 I got a production 500 scrambler from Hall Green. This was virtually the same bike that had been raced by Alan Bell and Mel Bayliss four years earlier, but it was an awful handler, and I only raced it a few times before trading it in for a new pick-up to replace our old Austin 10 van. I carried on racing the 250 up until the end of the 1961 season, when I decided to pension it off and replaced it with a 350cc Velo. I fitted it out with an Alfin barrel, BSA piston and an MAC Velo flywheel assembly, which gave it a long stroke of 68mm by 96mm, but it would rev beautifully. My first event on it was the Red Marley hillclimb at Easter in 1962, and I was delighted to get through to the final after I beat a Gold Star running on dope – regarded as one of the fastest 350s in the Midlands – in the semis. Alf Hagon won that final, but the Velo certainly gave a good account of itself, and during the rest of that season I had plenty of good rides on it. Of course, trying to keep it competitive took a lot of hours working on the bike during the week, and at the end of the year I had to make the choice of buying a new machine or packing it up. After racing for 15 seasons it was a hard decision to make, but by then I was 36 and fancied trying some new projects, so I sold the scrambler and made a Velocette-powered trials bike."

On the 250cc MOV-engined 'Barvel' special, Tommy would continue to compete in western and Wessex centre trials for the next 20 years, but the end of the '62 season brought the curtain down on the long and very successful scrambles career of one of the countries best postwar racers of his day: Tommy Barker.

The Bristol MCC team for the 1953 Wessex centre league trial. Tim is on the extreme left.

At virtually any major scramble back in the 1960s you could bet that the Westbury Motorcycles van would be there, and that Tim Pritchard would be cheering on one of his supported riders or doing a deal. Not a star in his own right, but a man who loved trials and motocross, Tim was at the epicentre of the 1960s motocross boom.

CHAPTER 7

TIM PRITCHARD – WESTBURY MOTORCYCLES

Free from the shackles of postwar austerity, the late 1950s and early '60s were great periods for the UK economy, and for individuals with entrepreneurial skills, drive and vision, business was booming. No more so than at 51-53 Westbury Hill in Bristol, which for three decades was the home to Westbury Motorcycles: the scramble world's Mecca. Founded in 1952 by local enthusiast Tim Pritchard, the story of Westbury and its rise from humble beginnings becoming to one of the biggest competition dealers in the country is a real 'rags to riches' one, and locals still recall a typical Saturday where the surrounding roads would be full of pick-ups and eager buyers.

To find out more about both his own riding career and the golden era in the '60s that saw a plethora of top men mounted on Westbury-sponsored bikes, I journeyed to north Somerset to meet the man who put the name of Westbury Motorcycles on the national map.

Now retired after a busy and successful working life, Tim and his wife, Margaret, live on the edge of the Mendip Hills. Their beautiful home is near to where, on a bleak winter's day in 1952, Tim competed in his first trial.

"After I came out of the RAF I got a job working for an insurance company in Bristol, and bought myself a 350cc BSA for the six-mile trip from my village home into the city. The job – viewed by my parents as 'one for life' – was mind-numbingly boring, and I spent most of my lunchtimes scanning the adverts in the local newspaper looking for another position. One, as a motorcycle salesman in Glanfield Lawrence caught my eye and, after a successful interview, I started there in March 1951. It only lasted until the November of the same year when I was summoned to the boss' office and given the sack; my 'crime' was knocking a fiver off the asking price of an old AJW. The bike was a heap and had been standing unloved in the showroom for several years, and with the boss away at the motorcycle show I was extremely pleased to have moved it on. I thought he would be delighted but his view was that I 'had broken company policy,' and as a result I was given instant dismissal and told to go downstairs and collect my cards."

Although he didn't realise it at the time, his dismissal from Glanfield Lawrence was just the spur he required, and within a few months Tim's embryonic new business at Westbury-on-Trym was up and running.

"When I was sacked I had about £100 in my bank account, so out of desperation I put an advert in the local paper, and from a friend's flat started buying and selling old prewar bikes. I could only buy one or two

47

Tim feet-up on the 500T Norton in the early 1950s.

Rob Taylor on the Westbury Metisse, May 1965.

at a time, but within a few months I'd prospered and by mid-1952 I had the chance to rent a very run-down property in Westbury; it cost me £4 a week, and Westbury Motorcycles was up and running.

"Bristol had been very heavily bombed during the war, and there were still a lot of damaged buildings around, but there was a sense of optimism in the air, and everyone it seemed wanted a motorbike. I had a natural ability to buy and sell all sorts of things but I badly needed a mechanic and in response to my advert in the *Bristol Evening Post* I was lucky enough to secure the services of Howard Janes. Howard had previously worked for Glanfield Lawrence and was regarded as one of their best men, but he'd left after discovering he was being paid a penny an hour less than his workmates. Despite his skills with the spanners the boss had refused to give him a rise, but their loss proved to be my gain, as he was a brilliant mechanic and we became lifelong friends."

With the business now flourishing, Tim was tempted into trying his hand at trials, which, as he later discovered would be the stepping stone to great things for Westbury Motorcycles.

"Other than the odd two-stroke Dot we'd had in the showroom at Glanfields I knew nothing about trials, but a friend persuaded me to have a go, and I bought myself an elderly 197cc James Commando. I remember little about those early events other than some bitterly cold winter mornings breaking ice as we rode along those deep gullies high up on the Mendips, but I gradually progressed, and by my second season I was on a 500T Norton. I picked up a few awards on the 500T, which saw me upgraded to an expert, but the fledgling business had

to come first, and as Saturday was our busiest selling day it meant I couldn't ride in the two big local nationals: the Kickham and the John Douglas. For these events the works teams would arrive a day or so before the trial for practice, which allowed me time to sneak off from work for a couple of hours and join them. It was fascinating to compare the styles of great riders like Gordon Jackson, Hugh Viney, Bob Ray, Geoff Duke, Bill Nicholson etc, and to sit in the pub at lunchtime and listen to their tales. They were in another league compared to me."

Keen to put into practice what he'd learnt watching the stars, Tim spent many hours negotiating the muddy banks on land owned by his friend and fellow trials rider George Fisher, and it was here in 1954 he got his first taste of riding a scrambler.

"George was a good, works-supported trials rider, but he fancied a go at scrambling so he'd built himself one around a 197cc Francis Barnett. In the early '50s there wasn't much money about, and as the bulk of the pukka factory competition bikes went for export, most of the machines the lads used in scrambles were little more than stripped down road bikes with wide handlebars, a noisy exhaust, and a pair of knobbly tyres. It was a similar machine – another 197cc Barnett – which a few weeks later I rode with my trade plate strapped to the rear mudguard ten miles to race in my first event. I loved it, and for the next 18 months or so combined both trials and scrambles; however, early starts on cold winter mornings began to lose its appeal, so I decided to concentrate on scrambling. By then I'd changed the Barnett for a 500cc Gold Star, but I quickly realised I was only an average centre rider, and I wasn't going to make a works team."

On one of the first production Challengers at Bleadon Hill, near Weston-Super-Mare, in 1964.

"IT WAS FASCINATING TO COMPARE THE STYLES OF GREAT RIDERS LIKE GORDON JACKSON, HUGH VINEY, BOB RAY, GEOFF DUKE, BILL NICHOLSON ETC"

ISDT action on the Husky in Italy, 1968.

Off-Road Giants!

Although Tim by his own admission was not an exceptionally talented rider, he was in the top league when it came to having an eye for business, and it wasn't long before the competition side of Westbury Motorcycles began to flourish and grow.

"Scrambling was booming, and there was barely a weekend when I wasn't out racing. At that time the major factories spent a lot of money fielding large works teams, and a win at a major event on Sunday resulted in plenty of road bike sales on the Monday. It also encouraged plenty of new riders into the sport, and the competition side of my business suddenly took off, which necessitated a move to a bigger showroom. Thanks to the contact I had with my local bank manager – we were both Bristol City football fans – I got the nod that the building which had formerly housed the Nat West on Westbury Hill was coming onto the market, and it would be perfect for my needs. I knew it was too good an opportunity to miss, so the deal was done, and after a couple of months of hard work the 'makeover' was finally finished, and our new premises was up and running."

Tim attributes the secrets of his business success to "being ahead of the game and always first with the new models, working seven days a week, plenty of good publicity, plus luck and timing." All of this was there in abundance, as the name of Westbury Motorcycles was broadened to a nationwide audience.

"On Sunday race days I was always talking to the lads and lining up deals, but one of my big sales breakthroughs came in 1955 when Cyril Quantrill started *Motorcycle News*, and this enabled us to go national with our advertising. Around the same time I also got involved with Cotton, who were just up the road in Gloucester. Monty Denly and Pat Onions ran the factory on a shoestring, but they were great people to deal with, and I put some money up to help them develop their new scrambler. We often had more jobs than our workshop could deal with, so, as they were glad to earn some extra cash, they helped us out by taking some of the repair work away to Gloucester and returning with it the following week in their ancient 'works' van.

"Virtually all the competition two-strokes at that time were powered by Villiers singles, but Cotton – like both Dot and Greeves – thought that the 2T twin had potential, and I collaborated with Pat Onions to build and race one. I quickly discovered that the 2T produced all the wrong sort of power for a scrambler, but I did have one memorable race on it. This was in the final of a very wet Yeo Vale meeting, and somehow my back wheel managed to find the only bit of grass on the start line and I shot off in the lead with all the two-stroke aces snapping at my heels. Prior to that I'd managed to win a few minor races and was usually a good starter, but I think my main problem was I wasn't strong enough to compete with the farmers and builders like Roy Bradley and Len Sanders, who dominated the local scrambles scene, and I would usually end up back down the order at the finish. My moments of glory were few, but on that day the track was both narrow and very slippery, and I managed to hold the lead for four laps before the Jarman and Sharp brothers got by and pushed me back to fifth at the finish."

Later, with riders like Billy Jackson, Fluff Brown and Badger Goss in the saddle of the Villiers-powered scramblers, and Colin Dommett a regular award winner on the works trials iron, Cotton expanded into a nationwide network of dealers, and predictably Westbury became one of the first. By the late '50s Tim had opened a second shop in the east side of Bristol, become an agent for Greeves, and also joined the MAA (Motor Agents Association); this, as he revealed, was an important stepping stone to becoming one of the industry's 'big boys.'

"I realised there was a dearth of dealers on the east side of Bristol, so when suitable premises came up I bought it and turned it into a motorcycle shop. By that time we'd made Westbury Motorcycles into a limited company, and Howard Janes – who managed the new shop at Staple Hill – had become a director. I'd also helped George Fisher – who was then riding for Greeves – with some stock for his new business, but after a while he decided to specialise in scooters, and as a pay off I became the Greeves agent for Bristol. This was perfect timing because riders like Stonebridge and Bickers had put the Thundersley two-strokes on the international map, and they were the bikes that everyone wanted.

"I'd applied to join the MAA, and it was ironic that when they sent someone out to inspect the premises it was my old boss from Glanfield Lawrence; the man who had given me the sack back in 1951! Thankfully he gave me the thumbs up, and the first new road bike we had in the showroom was a 98cc James, which came via Harold Fowler."

Away from the scrambles track, Westbury had also built up a useful trade with road-going sidecars, and it would be from this unlikely source that – via the golf course – doors would open to the top echelons of the motorcycle trade.

"Lionel – my friend and bank manager – had persuaded me to take up golf, and it was through this I got to meet the owner of one of the leading sidecar manufacturers. It transpired he was in the Reciprocal Golf Society made up of the top men from all the major motorcycle companies, and over the next two or three years this gave me numerous important contacts, which resulted in plenty of new bikes in our showrooms.

"The whole scrambles scene changed dramatically with the coming of the 1960s; there was a lot more money about, and the lads were able to buy new bikes and even pick-ups. The pudding basin helmet, battle dress and old fireman's boots of the '50s gave way to a variety of new helmets, leathers, coloured shirts, etc, and the old 'bitzas' gave way to pukka racing bikes like Greeves, Cotton, Dot, and the Rickman Metisse. Along with Comerfords and Hyland Crowe, we were by now one of the comp world's 'big three,' and every Sunday our van would be prominent at an important meeting somewhere within a 70-mile radius of Bristol. We were now sponsoring the Welsh champion Pete Atkinson on a Greeves, and, thanks to some great support from Derry Preston-Cobb and his works riders, we organised a demonstration day of their bikes at Doddington Park near Bristol. It was the first of its kind and at the end of a long but very successful day, we had a queue of people wanting a replica of Bickers' European championship-winning machine.

"'Cobby' – Derry Preston-Cobb – was a great character, and periodically I would make the long drive to Thundersley to see him and to twist his arm for more supplies. On arrival he could be guaranteed to provide plenty of laughs, and one day he couldn't wait to tell me how he'd been stopped and charged for speeding in his tuned invalid carriage on the nearby bypass. Greeves were super to do business with, and he and I would usually round the day off with a visit to the local Chinese restaurant."

Sunday race days not only gave Tim the opportunity to create contacts and line up deals, it also enabled him to spot and sign up-

Tim on the 400cc Husky motocrosser in 1970.

and-coming talent: men like Keith Hickman, Alan Clough, John Lewis, Rob Taylor, and the Devonian Dave Barnes, who all recorded numerous race wins on the Westbury-sponsored machines. Winter was a quiet time for scrambling, but he was acutely aware of the importance of keeping ahead of the game, and the advent of the Sporting and Racing Show saw the Bristol company taking centre stage in London's Horticultural Halls.

"In 1963 we made the front page in *MCN* with the news that John Burton had left the BSA works team and bought a Matchless Metisse from us, and the same year the first national show for off-road bikes was held in London. Up until then the only motorcycle show was at Earls Court, but for the one at the Horticultural Halls dealers were invited, and I could immediately see it had huge potential. We were the first booked in, and I managed to get the largest space which – thanks to one of our customers who was a shop fitter – we filled with a fantastic stand full of bikes, spares, and goodies; I have never worked so hard in all my life."

Tim and his team left the show hungry, thirsty, and exhausted, but it was undoubtedly a lucrative three days that left no-one in any doubt that Westbury Motorcycles was the market leader where scrambles bikes were concerned.

The following year would see them prominent at not only the sporting and racing show, but also at Earls Court, which, for the first time, featured a dealer's section. Once again, the Bristol company's glittering line-up – which included the newly announced mark three Metisse – stole the show, and this would set the scene for the rest of a busy decade, one in which Bultaco, Husqvarna, and a brace of Chris Horsfield's works CZs would in their turn all take centre stage.

Never one to rest on his laurels, Tim was always looking for ways to keep the name of his business prominent – all of his sponsored riders were entered on bikes that had 'Westbury' painted on their fuel tanks – and, working in tandem with his contact at *MCN* (John Phillips), they dreamt up a new, trendsetting advertising feature.

"Nowadays a two- or three-page feature with a write-up on the business and advertising by supporting manufacturers or suppliers is common practice, but it was something unheard of back in the 1960s. Nothing like it had been done before, which made it hard work getting the advertisers on board, but we persevered, and the end result was a four-page centrefold article by Gavin Trippe, which came out in October 1966.

"Gavin used a photograph of me with the newly opened Severn crossing in the background, and as a result I became known as 'The man who built the Severn Bridge.' I never lived it down, but it certainly helped us to sell lots of bikes."

The timing of the *MCN* article, the opening of the bridge, and the ever expanding motorway network brought a lot of customers to Westbury Hill, but Tim was still an active competitor himself.

"By the mid-'60s business was extremely good, and I'd taken on Colin Morton as sales manager. I was scrambling most Sundays, but I realised I was approaching 40 and decided that, before I was past it, I should try my hand at some of motorcycling's top events. I entered the '67 Scottish Six Days, and made my mind up that if I did okay would do the Welsh two-day trial in June and the international six days in September.

"I was probably a better trials rider than scrambler when I first started, but by then I'd been scrambling so long any skill seemed

to have deserted me, and I found those huge Scottish boulders too much of a challenge. I lasted to day three when the big end went on my Greeves, but I hadn't been enjoying myself, and it was a bit of a relief to retire. The Welsh, on the other hand, was superb, and it felt like it was designed for a scrambler. By then I was racing a 250cc Husqvarna in scrambles, and thanks to the tie-up we had with Brian Leask I ordered a 125 for the ISDT in Poland. I managed to secure a private ride through Cliff King – a friend in Bristol – and it opened up a whole new world for me.

"Just getting to the start via Czechoslovakia was an adventure in itself, but, other than a lost gearlever, the only problem I had in the trial was with a small screw which came loose in the carburettor. I thought I'd gone well prepared with enough spanners to fit everything, but it transpired that it was the one I didn't have, and I had to keep stopping to tighten it by hand. Luckily as I pulled up in the parc ferme Jack Stocker walked by and a spanner – which just happened to be the correct size – 'fell out' of his coat pocket, and with the screw securely tightened the little Husky never missed a beat for the rest of the event.

"Although the bike ran perfectly there was no way I could stay on time, not every check for six long days, but I managed to finish and got a bronze medal for my endeavours. To win a gold medal you obviously needed superb riding skills but so much more besides, concentration for seven or eight hours a day, resourcefulness, and sheer determination to press on regardless of conditions or what's going on around you. I don't think there could be any doubt that those who competed in the Trophy and Vase teams were the top men in our sport."

Smitten by the enduro bug, Tim would go on to compete in five more international six days – another bronze on a 250cc Husky in Germany in '69 his only other medal – but he would continue to ride in the Welsh on no fewer that 21 consecutive occasions. On a variety of machines – Greeves, Husky, Suzuki and Honda – his best result was a silver medal in 1968, but there were numerous other bronze performances and one special award presented by the organisers to celebrate his 21st ride in 1987.

As the '60s slipped into the 1970s, the weekly advert proclaiming "100 used scrambles bikes for sale" continued to run in *MCN*, and on the racetrack West Country man Rob Taylor gave Westbury its finest hour when he finished second to Bengt Aberg in the British round of the 500cc world championship at Farleigh Castle.

Much of the success of the Bristol dealership had been generated by its enthusiastic founder, who worked tirelessly seven days a week, but when Tim retired from scrambling in 1972, the competition side of the business started to drop off.

"For the best part of 20 years I had spent virtually every summer Sunday racing and doing deals, but by the early 1970s the British industry had collapsed, the Japanese had come in, and I must confess I lost a lot of interest and took my finger off the pulse. We continued to sell road bikes, but by then I was involved in other businesses, and had less involvement with the running of the motorcycle shop."

The business would drift on until 1983, when the lights in the showrooms at Westbury Hill finally went out for the last time; three golden decades in which the name of Westbury Motorcycles – 'The home of motocross' – reigned supreme.

Big thanks to Tim and Margaret for all their time and hospitality in reliving some wonderful memories from a golden era.

A quiet man from the south Midlands, Eric Chilton was for a decade one of the leading international six-day trial riders of his generation, and during his glittering career he won five gold medals, one silver, and one bronze on his big four-stroke twins.

CHAPTER 8

ERIC CHILTON – STAR OF THE ISDT

R iding a motorcycle 1200 miles across mountains, through bogs, streams, and forests in a race against the clock for six strength-sapping days was arguably one of the toughest tests in the world for both rider and machine, and not without good reason was the ISDT marathon labelled the 'Olympics of motorcycling.' It was undoubtedly the ultimate challenge of skill, endurance, and mechanical durability, and through the pages of the weekly Green 'un and Blue 'un the select few who won a coveted gold medal achieved nationwide recognition for their achievements. The list of postwar British greats is a long one, and alongside names like Viney, Giles, and Heanes is a quiet man from the south Midlands; one who between 1954 and 1965 rode in ten internationals, winning five golds, one silver, and one bronze for his efforts. His name was Eric Chilton.

Many years have now flown by since the former Triumph and BSA rider hung up his muddy Barbour suit, but, as I discovered, he still has some wonderful memories from those golden days. His first ISDT was in Wales in 1954, but, as he recalled, his competition career began three years earlier on an unlikely machine for one-day trials.

"When my national service finished in 1949 the Berlin airlift was on, which meant we had to wait a further two months in Iraq before

we were flown home. I'd never had any interest in motorcycles, but back home in England I needed some transport, and, as a car was out of the question, I bought myself a B31 BSA. I started buying *The Motorcycle* and *Motorcycling*, and after seeing pictures of the bikes being ridden through lots of mud it looked like lots of fun, so I decided to have a go myself. My first event was a mid-Bucks club trial, but after getting to section one, the mud looked much too deep to negotiate on my road-going B31, so I turned round and went home. It was obvious the BSA was totally unsuitable, but I was dead keen to have a go, and shortly after, a friend told me that there was a Triumph Trophy for sale in Leighton's – our local bike shop – and, as it was designed to go across a ploughed field, it would be perfect for my needs. I immediately felt at home on the big twin, and during the next two or three seasons started broadening my riding horizons to the south Midlands centre group trials, and was soon getting in the awards."

Success in the one-day trials soon had Eric and the Trophy headed for Llandrindod Wells and the 1954 international six days: an event that was a steep learning curve for the young Chilton.

"The entry was oversubscribed – thanks to some help from my boss, Bob, mine was accepted – but other than the '54 Welsh two-

On the 500cc Triumph in selection tests for the 1962 ISDT. (Courtesy Don Morley)

day my previous biggest event had been a one-day sporting trial, so I was very green regarding bike preparation. Riding on my way to the start – no car in those days – I had a puncture in the rear tyre and just about managed to limp on to Llandrindod Wells, where I met up with the Dunlop pairing of Dickie Davis and his mate, Tom. I didn't have a clue how to change a tyre, but I borrowed some levers from Triumph's Henry Vale, and in-between sipping whiskeys Tom and Dickie taught me how to do this all-important operation. The trial itself was very wet and muddy, and some of the hills were more suited to a one-day event, and real stoppers for the small capacity bikes and the sidecars. However, thanks to my one-day experience and the lovely power delivery of my Triumph twin, I just managed to keep to my time schedule. This was particularly difficult on the day two night section, where, at one checkpoint, I had to fight my way to the clock to avoid a penalty. The bike kept going extremely well, but the chain was taking quite a hammering, prompting Vic from Reynolds Chains to ask me 'How many links has it got?' Of course, I didn't have a clue, and when he returned with a replacement he was equally surprised to see that I didn't have a quickly detachable rear wheel; I replied that I didn't have one because at that time I didn't realise that such a thing existed."

Despite the difficult going – which resulted in many retirements with drowned electrics – Chilton and the big Triumph kept going until the end, and when the results were announced he was rewarded with the first of his five ISDT gold medals. Although the big oil, chain and sparkplug suppliers were on-hand with their wares, Eric – like virtually all of the competitors – had to cover all of his own expenses competing in the internationals. He recalled that for his first in 1954, the entry fee was a staggering £25 – this in the days when the average take-home pay for a skilled man was around £3 a week.

There was no Chilton in the starting line-up of the '55 event in Czechoslovakia, but a year later he was bound for Garmisch-Partenkirchen in West Germany, this time on a 650 Triumph.

Like many of the private entries, the bike was ridden to the start – a couple of days across Belgium and Germany – but in a difficult event, described by the period press as 'severe yet sporting,' the young Brit suffered a nasty crash on a gravel track, and, although he eventually managed to kick the bike straight, he was forced to retire. International politics in the form of the Soviet invasion of Hungary and the Suez crisis were behind the ACU's decision not to support the 1957 event in Czechoslovakia, but that didn't deter three hardy British privateers

As part of the Trophy team, Eric on his way to gold in the 1962 six days in West Germany. (Courtesy Don Morley)

"CHILTON AND THE BIG TRIUMPH KEPT GOING UNTIL THE END, AND WHEN THE RESULTS WERE ANNOUNCED HE WAS REWARDED WITH THE FIRST OF HIS FIVE ISDT GOLD MEDALS"

Wonderful backdrop to the 1962 international. (Courtesy Don Morley)

Off-Road Giants!

– Chilton, Glassbrook, and Oliver – from making the long trip to Spindleruv Mlyn.

"After the disappointment of retiring in Germany I was desperately keen to ride in Czecho, so I put an advert in the motorcycle paper requesting for anyone who was interested in going to the international and wanting to share the costs to please contact me. I had response from both Albert Glassbrook and Jack Oliver, and at the beginning of September the three of us, plus Albert's wife, three bikes and all our riding gear and spares were jammed into Jack's van and we made the long trip to our destination behind the Iron Curtain. Jack did all of the driving – memorable because of his remarkable sense of direction, and that he kept overtaking on double white lines – and we arrived at the Czech border on the morning of the third day. With barbed wire, gun emplacements, and a huge RSJ across the road it wasn't very welcoming, and it took a long time for all of the checks and formalities to be carried out. After changing some money we were told we could proceed, but were given strict instructions of 'no stopping and no photographs' as we made our way through an area made up of pillboxes and heavy fortifications. Later that day we stopped in Prague and brewed some tea on our primus stove in a bus shelter, and eventually arrived at the trials HQ around one o'clock in the morning."

The trial is one of the toughest on record, with the axle deep mud seeing many crashes and early retirements – including Glassbrook on day one and Oliver on day two – but there was no stopping the determined Chilton and his big 650cc twin.

"From the parc ferme we were immediately into deep muddy forest tracks, which would have been impossible had the organisers not cut down scores of pine trees and laid them down across the worst of the boggy areas. Despite the conditions the bike kept going incredibly well, but trying to keep to the time schedule was impossible, and on the Thursday the event came near to collapse at one particular steep and narrow climb up a muddy track in low clouds and heavy rain. More than 50 riders finished the day very late – by 6.30pm it was quite dark, and 24 riders were still unaccounted for – so in the end the jury was forced to cancel the penalties sustained on the most difficult sections. We came to the trial totally self-contained with all of our own spares and oil – we had to pay for our fuel – but after Jack and Albert retired they and Albert's wife supplied me with dry gloves, petrol, and plenty of much-needed encouragement at the checkpoints to keep me going. I'd lost too many time penalties for any hope of a gold or silver medal, but I was determined to finish, and despite running out of brakes on the last day's speed test the bike never missed a beat."

At the end of six strength-sapping days – in which he was the only British competitor and the only 650cc rider to finish – Eric came away from Czechoslovakia with a bronze medal and many memories of his first trip behind the Iron Curtain.

"Although extremely tough the trial was extremely well organised with plenty of hot food at the lunch stops, and the medical facilities – usually stationed near dangerous hairpin bends – were first class. During the trial itself I became so focussed on just getting through each day it was almost like I was suffering from some sort of tunnel vision, and although the Czech people were very friendly I had no time to take in much of what was going on around me. At the end of each day I was exhausted, but I was sharing a room with the journalist Vic Willoughby, which meant I was kept awake until the early hours with him typing out his reports. The trip back home – which I spent in an armchair in the back of Jack's van – was trouble free, but it took me several weeks to recover from those six hard days on the bike."

After a successful winter riding in one-day events and the Scottish Six Days, Garmisch was again the setting for the 1958 international, with Chilton coming to the start line on a works 650cc BSA.

"I'd received a telegraph from BSA saying 'Ring Perigo ASAP,' and on doing so I was asked by him if I would like to ride a works Gold Star in the ISDT. I was flattered and thanked him, but told Mr Perigo that I'd always ridden twins, and wasn't too keen on a single; with that he said 'We'll prepare one for you then,' and agreed to send a similar bike for me to practise on down on the train. Beige in colour, it looked a bit tatty, but it went like the wind – I later discovered it was the development bike for the Super Rocket – and two up would easily do the ton. The works bike was a de-tuned Road Rocket engine in a Gold Star frame, and although it wasn't particularly quick its lovely soft power delivery was perfect for that year's trial. Two of my team-mates – Brian Povey and Brian Martin – were forced out with machine problems early on, but my bike ran perfectly until the end of day four, when it suddenly started to misfire on one cylinder. I changed the plug and checked the points – all of which seemed to be fine – and managed to limp to the finish within my time schedule. Bert Perigo was equally mystified as to what the problem was, but in the ten minutes allowed for fettling in the morning I discovered a broken HT pick-up which was quickly replaced, and my BSA became a twin once again."

With Povey and Martin out it was a disappointing ISDT for the Small Heath team, but a highly satisfying one for Chilton, who registered his second gold medal with a flawless ride on the big BSA.

His impressive performance also caught the eyes of the selectors, and, despite the British manufacturers' decision to boycott the event – Henry Vale is on record as saying "We can't sell any bikes behind the Iron Curtain," – the following year he was back in Czechoslovakia as an official member of the British Trophy team. Based for the fourth time at Gottwaldov, the trial itself was less difficult than those previously held there, but a series of crashes and mechanical failures decimated the British team, and at the end of six hard days Chilton and Terry Cheshire emerged as the only two UK riders still un-penalised.

Gold number three for Eric, and as the '50s turned into the swinging '60s there would be two more and a silver before the rain-lashed event in the Isle of Man – and a rare retirement – brought the curtain down on Chilton's competition career in 1965. Twelve years in which the quiet man and his Triumphs covered many thousands of strength-sapping miles pursuing that dream of an ISDT gold medal. Eric Chilton – a great rider and an unsung hero from a golden age in motorcycle sport.

Many thanks to Eric for all of his time and hospitality reliving some of those glorious days.

Eric and the big Triumph get a helping hand in a Banbury Nobac one-day trial. (Courtesy Don Morley)

In his last international on the 500cc Triumph, on the rain-lashed Isle of Man in 1965. (Courtesy Don Morley)

On his factory Greeves, Husqvarna, and CZ two-strokes, Dave Bickers was a true superstar of the 1960s scrambles scene. His epic battles for supremacy with fierce rival Jeff Smith in the hotly contested wintertime *Grandstand* and *World of Sport* TV trophies will never be forgotten.

CHAPTER 9

DAVE BICKERS – SUFFOLK PUNCH

"Bickers dominates" was the headline in *The Motorcycle* after the British round of the 250cc world championship at Glastonbury in June 1962. At Britain's first lightweight motocross GP, the young man from Suffolk had left the rest trailing in the wake of his factory Greeves, leaving few in doubt that he was the best quarter-litre scrambler in the world. Having ridden the Greeves to European championship wins in 1960 and '61, it was a surprise when the Thundersly factory announced that, instead of chasing the newly-created world title, Dave Bickers would be staying at home in '62, and the British round at Higher Farm Wick would be his only outing that year. He might have been missing from the world stage, but for Dave, the '62 250cc British championship season was a highly productive one: not only did he scoop yet another ACU crown, his all-action riding style made him a favourite with a legion of Saturday afternoon armchair viewers.

As a lad celebrating my tenth birthday I was lucky enough to witness that wonderful day at Glastonbury, although little could I have imagined that, five decades later, I would be reliving it with the man who was one of my boyhood heroes. I met up with Dave at his beautiful home in Suffolk, where he began by telling me about his early days on two wheels and his first scramble on a 197cc Dot.

"My dad ran a garage repairing both cars and motorcycles, and although he didn't ride a bike himself his two mechanics were both keen motorcyclists, and after work they'd give me a pillion ride down through the village, leaving me to trudge two miles back home. I think I must have been aged about eight when I got to ride my first bike, a 1929 200cc Francis Barnett which someone had left at the garage as a deposit on a repair, and then forfeited when they couldn't pay the bill. We didn't have a television, so every Saturday night dad would go to a friend's house to watch his favourite show, and while he was out I got the Barnett fired up and rode it round the village for a couple of hours – I didn't dare stop it, because it was a pig to start when hot. There was also an old 500cc Norton in the workshop with its piston and carburettor missing so I decided to try and get it running again. After a lot of skinned knuckles I managed to fit a piston from an old Morris commercial onto the Norton's conrod, and hammered a Bowden carb onto the manifold. The main jet was too weak, which meant it wouldn't run above half throttle, but I had a lot of fun on it, and every dinner time I used to come home from school and ride it around the village for 20 minutes or so: it was a noisy old thing, but no one ever complained.

The perfect combination in the early '60s: Bickers and the works Greeves.

With Pete Smith in the chair at the Kickham trial, March 1962.

"Shrubland Park was only two or three miles away, and after being taken to watch a couple of scrambles I decided that when I was old enough I would get a bike and have a go myself. On leaving school I'd gone to work in dad's garage, so I saved my money, and when I was 16 bought myself a 197cc Dot, which cost me £132. My first competitive event was, in fact, an Ipswich club trial at Burstal, and later on that same year – 1954 – I entered a scramble at the same venue."

16-year-old Dave and the Dot were taken to the start in style, in his neighbour's Standard Eight van, and for the teenager it was a memorable debut. He won his heat, and later in the day finished a strong third in the final; this, after a race-long duel with a rider on a 500cc Matchless, which, as he told me, taught him a lot about racing in the mud.

"With all the hours I'd put in riding in the woods and fields at home I was pretty good at tackling slippery conditions, but of course there I was on my own, and it wasn't until that first race I realised that being too close to the rider in front was not a good idea, as I ended up with a face full of mud!"

It didn't take the talented young Bickers long to be upgraded to the experts' ranks, and during the next two or three seasons he notched up some memorable victories on the home-tuned Dot and a variety of other bikes that came his way. At this stage much of his racing was in his home centre, but it was time to spread his wings, and, following a win over works ace Brian Stonebridge at a major national meeting at Southend in 1957, he got a call from Greeves.

"In addition to the Dot I raced all sorts of bikes, including an ex-WD Matchless, a 350cc Jawa (which I couldn't keep in gear), and a brand new 500cc BSA Gold Star but my big break came when I beat Brian on my Dot in a big meeting at Southend. Two-stroke tuning was all a bit of a 'black art' back then, and I guess they must have thought I'd done something special to the engine on the Dot, because I got a call from Greeves asking if I would like a rolling chassis to put my motor in."

From the 1958 season onward Dave was supplied with a full factory bike from Greeves, and with his mentor, Brian Stonebridge, he was soon bound for Europe. His GP debut was also his first trip outside the UK, and is still well remembered by him as one where he almost didn't leave Dover, and which left him with a nasty taste in his mouth.

Aviating the big Matchless, which, unknown to Bickers, had been bored out to 600cc.

"WITH ALL THE HOURS I'D PUT IN RIDING IN THE WOODS AND FIELDS AT HOME I WAS PRETTY GOOD AT TACKLING SLIPPERY CONDITIONS"

On his way to fourth place at Imola in June 1964, on the new Challenger.

A very muddy TV scramble on the Challenger, in the winter of 1964.

"The year's first GP was in Belgium, and as Brian was going to Europe ahead of the race he told me to drive my pick-up to Dover and then unload my bike and box of spares and push it on to the ferry. He would be waiting with his car and trailer at the other side, and we would go on together from there. It sounded easy enough, but when I got to Dover I was asked for my carnet for the bike, which I didn't know anything about. It looked like my GP was scuppered before it had started, but fortunately an AA man came to my rescue and I managed to get the Greeves on board. I got off at Boulogne, but my troubles weren't over, because I then had to push the bike – with the box of spares balanced on the seat – off the ferry and up a steep slope. This was all much to Brian's amusement, as he was at the top of the slope shouting words of encouragement. In the GP itself I retired in the first leg when my gearbox broke – a common problem with Villiers engines in those days – and between races set about repairing it. It might have been a European championship but we were expected to do all our own mechanical work, and I finished it just before the second leg was due to start. I was desperate for a drink, so picked up the bottle of orange juice Brian had in the back of his Zodiac. I took a couple of gulps

before I realised it wasn't orange juice but pink paraffin. I rode the second leg burping paraffin, but had a pretty good ride, and with the Belgian crowd urging me on – although to begin with I thought they were waving their fists at me – finished third."

Up until the time of Brian Stonebridge's tragic death in October 1959, Dave and his lanky mentor travelled many thousands of miles together chasing championship points, and half a century on Brian is fondly remembered by his protégé.

"It was a great day for Greeves when they signed 'Stoney,' because not only was he a world class rider, he'd also learnt a lot about two-stroke tuning during his time at BSA. Much of what he did to the Villiers engine was by trial and error, but Bert Greeves had the foresight to install a home-made dyno in the Thundersly competition department, and Brian put this to plenty of good use testing the engines. He was a great bloke who helped me a lot, although much of what I learnt from him was from what he showed me as opposed to what he told me. When I first signed for Greeves I was slightly in awe of him, and when racing together I wasn't too sure if I should overtake or not; however, I did so in a race at Shrubland Park and he never said a

Head down to another win on the very fast and reliable Husky.

"I RODE THE SECOND LEG
BURPING PARAFFIN, BUT
HAD A PRETTY GOOD RIDE,
AND WITH THE BELGIAN
CROWD URGING ME ON –
ALTHOUGH TO BEGIN WITH
I THOUGHT THEY WERE
WAVING THEIR FISTS AT ME –
FINISHED THIRD."

An early outing on the 250cc twin port CZ.

word! When we started doing the GPs together I had a Morris Minor pick-up, and the agreement was that we would share the driving, but I quickly discovered Brian was more than happy for me to do most of his share as well. He was also reluctant to carry his suitcase down from our overnight hotel room, and it was often thrown out of the window onto the pavement below; luckily no one was ever hit by the flying missile.

"Mr Greeves – no one ever called him Bert – and his disabled cousin, Derry Preston-Cobb, were in charge at the factory, and were very straight and honest to deal with, although when it came to talk about money 'Cobby' always came out with the tale that 'things were tight.' They eventually agreed to pay me £1000 a year to ride for them, but much of this came from sponsors like Shell, and BP and I think if Mr Greeves and Cobby had had their way I would have ridden for 4d!

"Derry Preston-Cobb was a really nice bloke and despite his disabilities he would turn up at scrambles all over the country in his tuned Invacar. He tipped it over a few times on the arterial road, and he also had it catch fire when it was being filled with petrol at a garage in Southend. Because of his disability Cobby couldn't get out of the car so they had to spray him with foam, and he returned to the factory looking like Father Christmas!"

For the 1960 season Dave was asked by Bert Greeves to contest the whole of the 12-round European series, and with the factory's chief mechanic, Bob Mills, in his Morris pick-up, Switzerland was the destination for the first race. Despite difficulties finding the track at Payerne, the long grassy circuit was ideally suited to the Bickers riding style, and he ran out overall winner ahead of Swede Torsten Hallman.

It was the perfect way to start his year, and as the season progressed it was obvious to one and all that Bickers was in a class of his own, and if the bike kept running he was going to be crowned the 1960 European champion. Many thousands of miles were covered motoring around Europe in the little Morris pick-up, and, as he recalled, he was left very much to his own devices when repairing a broken engine.

"I carried a couple of bikes, my riding gear and a box of spare cranks and gears in the pick-up; the Villiers engine was always shedding gears, and between rounds I would strip and rebuild the engine in a lay-by at the side of the road. Most of the time I travelled in convoy with the BSA pair of Jeff Smith and Arthur Lampkin, and we had a friendly agreement that whoever won the race would pay for the evening's meal. It's funny, whenever I won a race my first thought was 'Oh no, that's going to cost me another £10 tonight.'

"The first time we went behind the Iron Curtain was quite an experience, although for a while it seemed like we might not get in to or out of East Germany. We got to Checkpoint Charlie, but there was some irregularity with our papers, and we couldn't get into the East or turn round and get back to the West. We were in no-man's land, so while the problem was being sorted Smithy got his kettle and primus stove out and brewed us a cuppa. Once inside we found the East was a very austere place with lots of secret police about, but all the locals were extremely friendly and waved at us as we drove through. There were very few private cars on the road, and our pick-ups were viewed with envy, but everyone was extremely honest and nothing was ever stolen. The East German currency was virtually worthless, so the people were very keen on western money to buy a few of the luxury goods available, and we got some extremely good exchange rates on the black market."

Denied of international sport, the motocross attracted a huge crowd – most of whom arrived in buses – and they were privy to a superb day's racing that saw Bickers and the works BSA duo at their best.

Despite the efforts of his BSA rivals, Dave was crowned European champion that year, and, just to display his dominance of the quarter-litre class, he repeated this again in 1961. The following year – 1962 – the 250cc class was given world status, but there would be no Bickers, as the decision had been made at Thundersly for him to stay at home and concentrate on the British championships.

"Mr Greeves was a happy man when I won the two European crowns, but before the new season started he said to me 'We've won it twice, we won't contest it this year.' Motoring and racing around Europe was extremely tiring, and at the time I agreed with his decision, but the bike was going well and I knew I could have won it again; looking back I think it was my biggest mistake!"

As he showed at Glastonbury, the combination of Bickers and the Greeves was a winning one, and not only did he run away with the 250cc home championship, he also led the British team to victory in the Trophy de Nations team event, and in the winter became a firm favourite with thousands of Saturday afternoon TV viewers.

Much of Dave's career was spent on two-strokes, but he also had some memorable outings on the works 500cc Matchless, which he took to Switzerland for the Motocross des Nations in 1962.

"I was keen to race in the Motocross des Nations team, but of course at that time Greeves only had a 250, so I approached Hugh Viney and he agreed to let me have a works 500cc Matchless. It was a bit too big for me, but it was a great bike and went like hell. First time out I finished third on it at Matcham's Park in the Hants GN, and could have possibly won if I hadn't had a collision with Derek Rickman which ripped the throttle off. I had some good rides on it during that '62 season, and before the team event AMC asked me to take it back to the factory for tuning. Assuming it was in tip-top order, the first time I rode it after its visit to Plumpstead was in practice in Switzerland, and it was disappointingly much slower than before. In the race one of the shock absorbers snapped, but because it was a team event I tried to keep going with the tyre rubbing on the mudguard, belching out blue smoke, but eventually the clutch burnt out and I was forced to retire. On my return to England I met up with AMC's works rider Dave Curtis at Hawkstone, who asked me what I thought of the bike. In reply to my 'Didn't go too well,' he smiled and said 'The 500 never did!'"

"What Dave knew and I didn't was that I'd been racing it with a 600cc engine, and, worried that it would be measured at the Motocross des Nations, the comp department had changed it for a 500cc barrel and piston. Towards the end of that season I rode the Matchless at a meeting in France, and against a strong field thought I'd done pretty good, finishing third, but I had to ride it hard, and in doing so I buckled both wheels. On returning to England I took it back to the factory to have them straightened, and thought that after my good ride in France I might get a slap on the back. Instead Hugh Viney was so disgusted that I'd bent their bike he took it back and I never saw it or rode for them again."

Away from the racetrack Dave and his father had opened a motorcycle shop in Coddenham, and there were plenty of eager customers wanting replicas of his race winning bikes. However, the '63 season began poorly for him with a string of breakdowns on the works Greeves, which prompted a visit to the Huskvarna factory in Sweden.

"I knew what the Husky was like from racing against Torsten Hallman in the internationals, so I went to the factory and bought

"AS HE SHOWED AT
GLASTONBURY, THE
COMBINATION OF
BICKERS AND THE
GREEVES WAS A
WINNING ONE"

myself a new three-speed 250. Back home I fitted it out with a pair of Greeves leading link forks, but after race testing them I reverted back to the standard Norton forks that Husky used. It was a very quick little bike, and the only problem I had was with the three-speed box, which had a tendency to jump out of gear." This was eventually overcome when the factory supplied Dave with the latest four-speed box, on which he won the 250cc British championship again that year. There was also the occasional outing on the latest works Greeves, but, keen to have a competitive bike in both 250 and 500cc classes, Bickers was looking eastwards behind the Iron Curtain for his next factory ride.

"Joel Robert was going really well on the works CZs, and he arranged for me to go to the factory for a test ride and to meet the competition boss Mr Jarrolim. The bike was great and I then sat down with the committee to discuss terms. We agreed I would have a 250 and a 360 plus spares and a mechanic, so to celebrate a bottle of very strong 'Slibovitch' was produced. It wasn't long before one of the mechanics fell asleep and another got up to go to the toilet, but opened the wrong door and fell down a flight of steps into the cellar. My chosen mechanic was Zdenic 'Sten' Polanka, who had ridden in the GPs himself, and also represented Czechoslovakia in the international six-day trial. As I quickly discovered he was superb at keeping the CZ in tip-top condition, and all I had to do was ride it. Both the 250 and 360 were lovely bikes to ride, and Sten knew all the little tricks, like mixing engine and diesel oil together to improve the damping in the front forks."

Dave took to the pair of CZs like a duck to water, and during the following seasons there was hardly a major event when the combination of Bickers and the Czech two-stroke wouldn't be fighting for the lead.

"CZs were keen for me to alternate between 250 and 500cc world championships from year to year, and I think my best year was in 1966 when I finished third in the 500cc rankings. They were fantastic bikes to ride, and in the six or seven years I raced them they were extremely reliable and robust. Away from the start there was never a need to use the clutch, and I never broke a single gear in hundreds of races."

These included Trophy and Motocross des Nations rides for the national team and both British and world championship rounds, with thousands of miles covered in Dave's new race transport: a 7-ton truck that the resourceful Bickers had converted into a mobile workshop, complete with kitchen and some army beds.

"After the Morris Minor, the truck was the height of luxury, but it soon got bogged down, and after the Motocross des Nations in Switzerland we had to wait for two days before we could get out of the mud and away from the circuit."

His tie-up with CZ also saw the Bickers business expanding when he became the UK's importer of the Czech two-strokes.

"CZ and Jawa were keen to expand their export markets, so I took on a big warehouse and soon had it full of bikes which I distributed to dealers under the new name of Bickers Imports. We sold thousands of them – mostly road bikes – but later on CZ decided to do their own thing from a base in Kings Lyn, so with an empty warehouse we took over a company selling motorcycle parts as Bickers-Anglia Accessories."

Away from the hurly burly of international motocross and running an expanding business, Dave found time to ride in the occasional winter trial, and was good enough to win the Suffolk Mardle trophy event in two consecutive seasons: first on a Greeves solo, and the following year on a similar bike with a sidecar attached.

However, his first love was scrambling, and throughout the 1960s

Bickers and the works CZs were a regular feature in both the British Trophy and Motocross des Nations teams. Across the Atlantic motocross was booming, and, keen to attract the world's best, the Trans-Am series was founded, and in 1970 Dave found himself stateside. The pay was good, and Dave was just one of a bevy of international stars, including Joel Robert and his CZ team-mate Chris Horsfield, who over the course of the next three seasons brought world class motocross to the USA.

Right up to the mid '70s Dave was still capable of finishing in the top ten at British championship events, but after an incident in Wales he decided it was time to retire from major events.

"I still loved racing in the championship events, but one day I was passed in mid-air by Dave Watson, who went by like I was stood still, and I decided there and then it was time to retire from top class racing. I continued to ride in France and Belgium for fun, and also did two international six-day trials. The first one was in Czechoslovakia, and I was on gold medal schedule up until the last day when it poured down with rain. The tracks turned into a sea of mud which blocked the fins on my PE 250 Suzuki causing it to overheat, and I had to keep stopping to change cooked plugs. In the end I was outside my hour time allowance, so came home with nothing. My second ISDT was in Sweden on a 360cc KTM, which ran perfectly for the whole week, although I thought I'd blown my chances of gold on the final day's special test. It was laid out on a very flat field, in which, to make things a bit more difficult, the organisers had dug some extremely deep holes. Had it stayed dry they wouldn't have been a problem, but it poured with rain and the course turned into a mud bath. I remember flying over the handlebars, and all around the long lap wood was being pulled out of the forest to try and make something solid to ride across. I was almost in tears through my efforts manhandling the KTM and thought I'd blown my chances again, but because it had turned into such a fiasco the organisers decided to cancel the special test and I won a gold medal."

It was Dave's second and last ISDT, although certainly not the end of his motorcycling career. He continued to scramble right up until the late 1980s, and he was also the man to whom film companies came when they wanted stunts arranged.

"The stunt thing came about almost by accident after a film company asked me if I could get someone to jump a WW2 sidecar outfit over a washing line in Greece. Over the years it's gone from strength to strength and is now run by my son who goes all over the world with his team arranging all sorts of stunts for movies."

The love of motorcycling runs deep within Dave Bickers' veins, and although his racing career is now long over he usually has a rebuild or two under way in his well-equipped workshop and with a group of friends he still enjoys a weekly ride along the Suffolk green lanes on his little Beta Alp.

The quiet unassuming man from Suffolk was undoubtedly one of the greatest scramblers of his generation, and it was a privilege to record some of his memories of that golden era to print.

Dave Bickers 1938-2014

It was sad to hear that Dave – the quiet, unassuming man from Suffolk – passed away at the beginning of July 2014. He was one of the true greats of the 1960s scrambles scene, and, for those of us lucky enough to have seen him in action, memories of the Coddenham flyer will live forever.

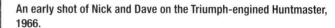
An early shot of Nick and Dave on the Triumph-engined Huntmaster, 1966.

A man who went from racing on a shoestring budget funded by a group of friends, to taking on and beating the best in the rough and tough world of sidecar cross on his Ken Heanes-sponsored Wasp outfits.

CHAPTER 10

NICK THOMPSON – SIDECAR SUPERSTAR

Our story begins on a bitterly cold day at Biggin Hill in February 1962. As the tape flies back the sidecars are away for their first four-lap heat of the new season. Among the field of booming four-strokes is an old 500cc Matchless/Watsonian outfit ridden by Nick Thompson and his passenger Dave Beavis: two keen and enthusiastic teenagers making their racing debuts. It was a tough initiation to the art of sidecar scrambling for the young duo, who quickly discovered that negotiating muddy slopes and adverse cambers was no easy task on a bike that had a desire to go anywhere other than in a straight line. There were no trophies, prize money, or the popping of champagne corks that day at Biggin, but in the future there would be plenty of celebrations for Nick, who, along with Beavis – and later Mike Ripper, Peter Logan, Gary Withers, Barry Williams, and Chris Herbert as ballast – became one of the greatest home grown charioteers of his generation. Between 1967 and 1980 he would be crowned four-time British champion, eight-time runner-up, and only once in those 14 seasons would he be out of the top three, this in 1971, when he finished runner-up in the inaugural FIM Cup and missed several of the British rounds.

To find out a little more about those early days when he and his friend Dave raced on a shoestring budget, up to the championship winning seasons on the Ken Heanes-sponsored Triumph and Norton-engined Wasps, I met up with Nick and his wife – and number one fan – Pam, at the home they share in West Sussex. Nick takes up the story ...

"I was born and brought up in London, and it was here I got my first taste of racing when, along with seven or eight of my mates, we formed the Zebra's cycle speedway club. In chequered shirts my mum made we used to race against other teams, and this was how I met and got friendly with Dave Beavis. My dad had no interest in motorcycling, but one of our neighbours, Jack Smith, was a keen member of the Sunbeam club, and on leaving school my parents bought me my brother's 197cc James – a road-going scrambler – to get me to my work in Acton. I started there as a trainee draughtsman – very boring, as I did little else than make the tea – and it was through meeting a fellow worker, Johnny Higgs, that I bought the Matchless sidecar outfit for £10. Along with Pam and several of my friends I'd cycled to spectate at a few scrambles at Pirbright and Biggin Hill, and had noticed that, although there were plenty of solos, there were precious few sidecar entries, so with Dave volunteering to be passenger we decided to get the Matchless ready for race action. It was a 500cc road bike with teles on the front and a rigid rear end attached

Plenty of style from Nick and Dave Beavis on 007.

to a Watsonian VG21 chair, and by the time we'd finished 'preparing' it with scaffolding boards on the floor it weighed a ton. One of our friends, Mick Spurling, had a 5cwt three-speed Morris van, so to get to the meeting we removed the front seat, took the rear wheel out of the bike, and detached the chair – which was strapped to the roof – and eight of us managed to squeeze in alongside the Matchless. We were full of enthusiasm, but the shortcomings of our bike – with its heavy chair – were soon evident, and in our heat we were still struggling to complete our first lap when the winner crossed the finishing line. We had no money to get anything more competitive, and it's thanks to our six friends who chipped in 2/6d each a week we managed to keep the bike running during that first season. The motor was very tired, and the Burman gearbox kept breaking, but things started to improve when we got another 500cc Matchless engine from a complete bike we

found in a skip, and in '63 we won our first prize money. We were at the Rushden circuit, which featured lots of adverse camber and a mud hole with a stream running through it. Many of the outfits got bogged down in the mud, but, with help from our mates, Dave and I managed to keep moving, and we were up to third in our heat when the chain snapped. We thought that that was the end of our day's racing, but it transpired that only two other outfits had finished, so as we had been running third the organisers invited us to line up in the final. Again there were plenty of breakdowns, and when the chequered flag fell we were one of only three outfits still circulating: we won ten shillings for third place, and felt like millionaires!"

It was during that tough 1962 season that Nick first raced against Mike Guilford – a man who later in the '60s would become one of his fiercest rivals – and he also got some gas welding gear to make his first

Thompson and Beavis in France, where they finished winners in their first GP.

Two wins for Thompson and Beavis, Dutch GP, 1971.

Closely watched by sponsor Ken Heanes at Foxhounds.

sidecar: a lightweight chair attached to a replacement for the 500cc Matchless. He takes up the story again ...

"We needed to have something more competitive, so I sold the Matchless back to Johnny Higgs for £11 and replaced it with a 650cc Ariel Huntmaster. A chap near my home in London had given me some welding gear, so I made up my own sidecar chassis, which I decided to name after James Bond and called it the '007.' It was about half the weight of the one we'd had on the Matchless, but sadly the big Ariel didn't take too well to being revved hard, and at the second meeting the engine went bang in a big way. I then got an old 650cc Triumph engine from Dennis Ethridge for £10, but quickly discovered it was clapped out and we had to fork out another £30 to get it rebuilt; this done by a little engineering company in Ealing, who also made the new engine plates to fit it into the Huntmaster frame. Both Dave and I – along with our two wives – were getting pretty disenchanted, and seriously thought about packing it in, but when Dave Fox got to hear about it he gave us a hell of a rollicking and we quickly changed our minds. He also gave us some good advice on the use of 'Nyloc' nuts and Allen bolts to hold the engine and frame together, and with a bike which was by now fairly quick and reliable we started going places. For the first two seasons all of our racing was in Sussex and Kent, but as Dave and I started to improve we joined the Portsmouth club to race in the Hampshire centre – a popular one for the sidecars – and in '65 we decided to do some selected rounds of the newly announced British championship. I was aware that we needed to improve the bike's handling, so in readiness for the championship races I replaced the original telescopic front forks with a set of strengthened leading links, which had originally been fitted to a Douglas Dragonfly. I now had a Ford 100E van which towed a big trailer with the outfit on to events all across the country, but sadly the old three-speed side valve engine was hard pushed to deal with steep climbs; especially when it was raining and the vacuum operated windscreen wipers would stop working."

The modification to the front end certainly improved the way the bike steered, and people were starting to sit up and take notice of the Thompson/Beavis combination who were by now challenging the established sidecar stars and picking up regular championship points on their home brewed Triumph-engined special. 1966 saw Nick and Pam

move to Bognor Regis. A good move, as not only was their solicitor good at his chosen profession, Roy Gardiner was also a very keen motorcyclist and the man who would later become Nick and Dave's race manager dealing with all of the entries and paperwork when they began to compete in the FIM, European and world championships. However, that would be in the future; Nick picked up the story again in '66 and told me about their new race transporter, along with a memorable incident from Newbury when they were lucky to make the start.

"We'd pensioned off the old and very slow 100E and replaced it with a 15cwt Thames, which we purchased for the princely sum of £65 from the Plastic Moulding Company in Brentford. By now we were doing most of the British championship rounds, so not only was the van our race transporter, it was also, on occasions, our overnight accommodation. It was a bit rough and ready, but we were having to race on a shoestring budget, and of course there was no money available for luxuries like a bed and breakfast. My Triumph-engined outfit was now going pretty well, but during practice for a championship round at a very wet Newbury, one of the main chassis members on the sidecar fractured, and it looked like we were going to be non-starters. Thankfully someone gave us the tip-off that there was a small workshop open in the town, so we chucked the bike into the trailer, and, dodging all of the spectator traffic coming into the meeting, we sped off into Newbury, where we got it welded up and still managed to get back to the track in time for the first race."

For both 1966 and '67, the British title was won by the pairing of Len Crane and John Pearson on their 'Cranwar' outfit, but they had to contend with plenty of fierce opposition from not only the experienced crews like the Price and Rose brothers, but also young pretenders in the form of Guilford and Malcolm Lambdon on the new RTGS – later to be renamed the Wasp – Bob Nash and Trevor Jones, and the ever improving Thompson and Beavis duo on their home-brewed Triumph special. The lightweight but super strong Wasp became the bike to beat, and Guilford's title win in 1968 would be the first of 14 successive British championship wins for the Wiltshire company. Not that Guilford had an easy time for his title wins in '68 and '69, as each round he was harried every inch of the way by Thompson, and there were some memorable wins for the Sussex-based man. Among them was the day at Harcombe Bottom, where an audacious overtake through a gorse bush in the heat was repeated again in the final, to see Thompson and Beavis first past the chequered flag.

Sidecar racing was becoming extremely popular in both the UK and Europe, so it came as no surprise when the sports organising body announced the inaugural FIM Cup in 1971. As runners-up in the British championships three years on the trot – '68, '69 and '70 – Thompson was one of the first names to go into the hat as one of the three British riders eligible to compete for the prestigious trophy. It would be the start of a memorable decade that saw the British star travelling thousands of miles in pursuit of FIM Cup, and, later, European and world glory on his Triumph and Norton powered Wasp outfits: bikes that, as he recalled, were sponsored by a very generous Ken Heanes.

"I now had a Wasp powered by my pre-unit Triumph twin engine, but I was aware that to be competitive against the best sidecar racers in the world the motor needed to be in tip top condition, so during the winter I phoned Ken Heanes and asked him if he would tune it for me. Throughout his long career in both scrambles and the international six-

Race action on the fast but heavy T150 Triumph Wasp in '72.

Dave Beavis keeping the third wheel down at Brighton in 1973.

day trial Ken had always ridden Triumphs, and as his shop was one of the biggest in the country for Meriden twins I figured he was the perfect man to get my motor running at its best. He said he would be more than happy to tune it, but much to my surprise a couple of weeks later he phoned me to say 'your engine's ready.' I couldn't quite grasp what he was telling me because my engine was still in my workshop and I hadn't yet delivered it to him, but he then went on to say 'I've got one here for you; I'm going to sponsor you.' When I went to pick it up I was delighted to see it was one of the latest 650cc unit construction twins fitted with one of Vale Onslow's 750cc conversions and fuelled by a big single Amal carb. I went back to Wasp for some new engine plates, and once fitted I raced it in a couple of early season meetings to give it a shakedown before the big first race in France; needless to say it ran like a dream. At that time I was working as a plater/welder for a small company in Sussex, and was delighted when my boss readily agreed to let me have Fridays and Mondays off so I could have plenty of time to travel to and from the European meetings.

"The '71 championship opener was at Pernes Les Fontaine near Marseille; it was the first time I'd been abroad, and Roy Gardiner had taken care of the entries and ferry bookings in his usual efficient manner. I was then using a 1500cc mark one Ford Cortina estate as my tow car, and although it was a bit thirsty – around 20mpg – petrol was cheap, and it seemed like the perfect vehicle to cover the 800 miles from Calais down to Marseille. The plan was to take a late evening ferry from Dover to Calais and cover the bulk of the miles overnight, and arrive with plenty of time to get accustomed to the conditions and have a rest before the three half-hour plus two-lap races on the Sunday. Sadly, in the dark the lights gave up the ghost, and we had to sleep in the car and wait until daylight before we could trace the fault to

a broken earth wire and get on our way again. It rained virtually the whole way, and the long delay meant that we didn't arrive at the circuit until late, and the three of us spent the night sleeping in the grandstand. By race day the rain was gone, and with a dampened track it was perfect conditions for racing. A typical sidecar race at home would see perhaps 15 outfits come to the start line, but Dave and I were just one of 45 from all across Europe who came under starters orders for that first FIM championship race. We had a decent ride and finished fifth in the first leg, but Dave was always on the lookout for ways of getting an advantage, and he'd noticed that when it was released the mechanical start gate dropped into a channel, and as we lined up for race two he told me 'When you see that bar move, go.' I followed his instructions to the tee and we got a terrific start, and spent the whole of the race locked in a terrific battle with Hallers on his big Honda four. We eventually finished runners-up to him, but in the next, final leg his chain broke and we went on to win; this made us overall victors, and we went away with what at the time seemed like a fortune of £128 in prize money."

That win in the south of France was the prelude to a wonderful season for the British pair, who followed up with a second in Germany and two wins in the strength-sapping sand in Holland. Nick regards the victory in the Dutch GP – where in the second race he overtook Rik Lubers in mid-air – as one of the greatest of his long career, and over 40 years later he is still the only Brit to ever register two straight wins there. The cut and thrust of top class sidecar racing certainly caught the imagination of the crowds, which lined the circuits all around Europe to witness Thompson and Lubers fight for that coveted FIM crown; a fight that went down to the wire, with the talented Dutchman narrowly fending off his fierce rival to scoop the title. It was also a notable championship for Robin Rhind-Tutt, as not only were Lubers and Thompson mounted on his outfits, but the first seven places were all filled by Wasps. Concentrating on the FIM Cup meant that Nick missed several of the home championship rounds that year, but he still managed to finish a creditable fourth on his Heanes-sponsored Triumph Wasp. There are enough tales from the ten years he competed in the FIM, Euro, and later the world championship races to fill a book, but, as Nick was quick to acknowledge, his successes couldn't have been achieved without the generosity of the man who sponsored him: Ken Heanes.

"Not only did Ken supply us with engines, spares and rolling chassis, he also arranged additional sponsorship from Duckham's oil, Regina chains, Melton goggles and Champion spark-plugs; a terrific setup, which meant that, with Roy looking after all of our entries, all I had to do was to ride the bike. Other than that first season with the Matchless and Ariel, all of my racing had been done with Triumph twins, but for 1972 Ken thought that it would be a good idea for us to try a T150 triple in our Wasp chassis. It was reasonably quick, but much heavier than our old engine, and we could never get the suspension to work properly, so after half a season we gave up and reverted to our old twin. Our first outing was at the French GP where we suffered a seizure in practice – sand had somehow found its way into the oil-carrying frame – and we had to strip and rebuild the red hot engine before the first race. It was a great team effort to get it ready, and we were rewarded with a fourth in race one and fifth in the second leg."

It was one of the highlights in Europe, where they only managed to finish ninth in the final standings, and in the home championship they were again runner-up; this time to John Turner and Nick Meredith on

Aviating the 750cc Norton Wasp at Frome in '74.

"I WAS DETERMINED NOT TO GO DOWN WITHOUT A FIGHT, SO I DECIDED TO CUT OFF THE PLASTER OFF AND STRAPPED THE LEG FOR THE RACE"

With Gary Whithers in the chair of the 920cc Norton Wasp.

another Triumph-engined Wasp. It looked like Thompson and Beavis were destined to be the perpetual 'bridesmaids,' but this all changed with a new engine in '73 and a run of three consecutive championship titles for the talented Sussex man. Nick takes up the story again ...

"Ken had managed to get an ex-works 750cc racing engine from Norton, and although we had to modify it a little to get it to pull it was a fantastic motor. It hardly missed a beat all season, but the rigours of sidecar racing gave the standard gearbox a hard time, and as a safeguard we used to change all of the gears every six meetings. Later on Ken supplied us with a four-speed set of Quaife gears, which were specially designed for racing, and with a bullet proof ultra-reliable engine we ran away with the British championship that year."

For the rest of the decade – along with his talented passengers Beavis, Withers and Chris Herbert (Ripper and Logan were stand-ins during '76) – Thompson on the Heanes-sponsored Norton Wasps registered hundreds of wins in both the UK and Europe, in which thousands of miles were covered chasing precious championship points. Most of these were trouble-free, but, as Nick recalled, there was one very nasty incident in which they were lucky to escape uninjured.

"Dave was a brilliant passenger and a great friend but after 13 hard seasons he decided to call it a day at the end of the '75 season – our third title win – and after a handful of races with Mike Ripper and then Peter Logan in the chair the following year, Gary Withers became my regular ballast. I'd tried him out at Boscombe Down on a piece of land used by Mike Guilford for testing, and could see from the outset he was a natural. Our first race together was the British round of the European championship at Halstead, where we registered two third places to take second overall. We had a good season in both the British, where we finished second behind the big Yamaha of Terry Good and Jess Rixon, and also in Europe, where we were third. To keep the travel costs down for the Euro rounds we often took John Turner along with his passenger and bike with us in our van and trailer, and would meet up with Gary at Dover for the onward trip. For the '76 German GP at Erbach we left home at 3.00am, but were only around an hour or so into our journey when on a long straight I spied a big van coming the other way. I was aware that he was taking up a lot of our side of the road so pulled onto the verge; what I didn't know was that the driver had fallen asleep at the wheel, and although we were stationary he smashed into our van and ripped the back panel off. No one was seriously injured, but our race transport was now out of action, and in the days before mobile phones I had no way of contacting Gary. I did, however, manage to get to a phone and spoke to my friend Johnny Hughes, who arrived with another van, and with bikes, spares and riding gear all transferred we were on our way again. We were six hours late arriving at Dover, but thankfully Gary was still waiting for us."

After finishing runners-up in the British championship in both 1976 and '77 Nick scooped his fourth – and last – title in 1978; one that, as he recalled, went down to the wire between himself and the hard-riding Doug Fox.

"Throughout that year there was only a few points separating Doug and myself, and going into the penultimate round at Miserden Park in Gloucestershire I was holding a slender lead. As the race got under way we got embroiled in a great dice for the lead, but going into a sharp right-hand turn we collided, and in the ensuing melee I ended up with the outfit on top of me and a broken ankle. Doug went on to win and now led the championship, while I was out of action and on my way to hospital where the ankle was put into plaster. With only two weeks until the last round it looked like my championship hopes were well and truly scuppered, but I was determined not to go down without a fight, so I decided to cut off the plaster and strapped the leg for the race. My mechanic, Dave Coates – a brilliant man with the spanners – and Gary prepared the bike, and although I could only hobble around I felt pretty good as we lined up for the first race. What I didn't know was that the previous weekend Doug had raced in a non-championship event in France where he'd crashed heavily and ended up with a badly bruised leg, which made riding his bike almost impossible. As the gate dropped I got a fantastic start and led into the first corner; John Roberts was lying second, but had a big spill which held the rest of the field up, and I led from start to finish, lapping Doug, who had lost all of the feeling in his injured leg."

Although he finished runner-up in the race for the British title in both 1979 and '80, they were two mediocre years in the European and newly announced world championships, and the following year Nick decided to retire from the internationals. He did, however, carry on competing in the UK, on a bike very different from his booming Norton four-stroke twin.

"The Yamaha importers asked me to race one of their air-cooled 500cc two-strokes in the sidecar support championship, so I built an outfit, and after luring Dave out of retirement decided to give it a go. The power delivery was very different to the old Norton, but I soon got accustomed to it, and although we didn't compete in all of championship rounds we won the title that year. I was still doing the odd non-championship international race, and it was in one of these in Germany we suffered a big crash. We came together with a right-hand chair and I ended up with two broke vertebrae, two broken ribs, and a two-week stay in a German hospital. I'd been racing every season with little in the way of serious injuries since 1962, and had a wonderful career, so I decided it was time to retire."

However, the lure of competition is hard to resist, and two years later Nick was persuaded to compete in an 'old timer's' race in Holland. He finished a creditable third on Norman Gale's 1000cc Yamaha, and at the end of the year he also competed in the first Weston beach race where, at the end of three strength-sapping hours, he was fifth on the same bike. 1985 was Thompson's last appearance in the British championships, and although by then he was past his best, he still recorded some decent top five finishes on a very quick 500cc water-cooled Honda/Wasp two-stroke. At the end of a hard season he was eighth in the standings, but he realised it was time to finally call it a day. The helmet and leathers were hung up for the last time, and the curtain fell on the career of one of the sidecar world's true greats: Nick Thompson.

Big thanks to Nick and Pam for their time and hospitality, and for reliving some memories from a golden era.

From the village lad riding pillion on his father's trials bike, to the man who became one of the UK's leading motocrossers on his Westbury Motorcycles-sponsored Husqvarna, Rob was the crowd's favourite the day he almost beat the best in the world.

CHAPTER 11

ROB TAYLOR – BAKER'S BOY TO SCRAMBLE STAR

"Taylor's glory" was the headline after the British round of the 500cc world championship at Farleigh Castle in the summer of 1970. Three tough and gruelling races where against the best in the world local star Rob Taylor and his Westbury sponsored Husqvarna finished a magnificent runner-up to Bengt Aberg; the Swede who was on his way to his second world crown. With three busy motorcycle shops to run, the talented West Countryman was only a part timer on the world stage, but as he proved on that memorable day, he was one of the best home-grown scramblers of his generation. On a variety of machines which included Cotton, BSA, Metisse, Husqvarna, AJS, Maico and KTM's Rob raced for 20 highly successful seasons; a passion for off road sport which as he recalled was kickstarted into action at an early age.

"My parents owned the bakery and shop in the village of South Brewham in Somerset, which was a fantastic place to be raised. As a child I would help out with odd jobs like filling the farmer's tractors with fuel from our solitary pump, and accompany dad on his round delivering the bread, which meant I got to know lots of people. It seemed that my parents were working 24 hours a day, but dad loved motorbikes, and when I was aged about eight or nine he bought a

Triumph trials bike from Jim Alves. Most Sundays in the winter he was out riding in local events, so as I was keen to go with him he rigged the Triumph up with a sponge pillion seat. This meant he could carry me between sections, where on arrival I would jump off and run up through to the end's card, where, after he'd ridden it, he would pick me up and take me on to the next one."

Bitten by the motorcycling bug, Rob was keen to have a go himself, but had to wait until his 16th birthday in 1960 before he could tackle the Wessex centre mud on a Greeves Scottish. Although, as he revealed, his 'unofficial' debut had come the previous year in a Somerton club time and observation trial.

"By 1959 the Triumph had been swapped for a Sun two-stroke, which dad had entered in a time trial at Steart Hill. He signed on and started, but after two laps pulled in and, with me kitted up, handed it over, and I completed the rest of the trial; the secretary of the meeting, Dave Jenkin, knew what we'd done, but turned a blind eye to the fact I was only 15. My dad was very keen for me and my brother Brian to follow his footsteps into trials, and when I reached my 16th birthday he bought me a Greeves Scottish. Two years older than me, Brian was already riding and looked a natural – he later became Wessex champion

A rare picture of Rob on the factory 250cc Francis Barnett, which failed to finish a race.

– but although I picked up a couple of novice awards, I was a bit too much gung-ho to be a decent trials rider, so decided to put a pair of knobblies on the Greeves and do a few local scrambles."

One of these early outings was on the steep slopes of Yarley, where the young Taylor was soon impressing riders and spectators alike with his smooth yet tenacious riding style. It was obvious that with a decent bike he had huge potential, and it wasn't long before he'd registered his first win, and was upgraded to the ranks of expert with his newly acquired Cotton.

"The Greeves trials bike had a hammering riding it in scrambles, so I exchanged it for a new 250cc Cotton from Fred Wiggins; it was a great little bike and got some good results, including my first race win at Somerton. On leaving school I'd gone to work in the family business, which meant that I couldn't go too far from home to race as I had to get back for an early morning start in the bakery, therefore, most of my racing at that time was limited to fairly local events. One of these was at the Frome club's Leighton circuit, where in 1962 I lined up on the Cotton for a heat of the Rob Walker trophy. I was alongside Don Rickman, who nodded his head and smiled at me as we waited for the start. I can't remember much about the race now, but that acknowledgement from one of my great scrambling heroes made my day, and I remember rushing back into the pits to tell my dad about it."

At the start of the '63 season the Cotton was traded for an MCS Greeves, and there was barely a meeting in the south of England where the name of Rob Taylor didn't feature in the results. Some stunning rides during that season also impressed motorcycle journalist Chris Carter, and, as Rob recalled, this led to his first works machine and a long trip north to Birmingham.

"Chris Carter had written some complimentary words about me, and when he was covering the big events in the West Country he used to stay overnight in our house in South Brewham. My everlasting memory of Chris is his old Ford Anglia, which was incredibly rough and littered with half-eaten sandwiches and empty crisp packets. On one of his visits he asked me if I fancied a ride on a works James, and gave me the number of the man I needed to speak to; this was Hugh Viney, who invited me to go to the AMC factory in Birmingham. I then had a Morris Minor pick-up, and in the pre-motorway days Birmingham seemed like the end of the earth away, but I eventually found the huge AMC factory and was directed to Mr Viney's office. He took me to the comp shop where I met another of my heroes, Chris Horsfield, working on his works Matchless, and there was my sparkling new James which Viney told me to 'take back to Somerset and tell us what you think of it.'"

Sadly, it didn't take Rob too long to formulate an opinion on the works bike, which in his hands failed to finish a race.

"My first meeting on the James was at Tog Hill near Bath, but it only lasted a few laps when the gearbox broke and flew out through the case. The following day I phoned Hugh Viney who told me to take it back to the factory, but of course this meant that my father had to do all my work in the bakery while I was away. On arrival at the AMC plant

West Country race action on the Westbury-sponsored Triumph Metisse in 1966.

"I CAN'T REMEMBER MUCH ABOUT THE RACE NOW, BUT THAT ACKNOWLEDGEMENT FROM ONE OF MY GREAT SCRAMBLING HEROES MADE MY DAY"

On the works AJS Stormer in a TV scramble.

Viney told me I had to go to the Villiers factory where they would sort me out a new engine, and with this fitted I was reasonably optimistic that it might be competitive and reliable. Unfortunately my next race only lasted a few laps before the engine seized solid; I was totally disheartened, and that was the end of a very short session as a works James rider."

For the next two seasons Rob continued to race his own Greeves, but he was keen to perform on a 'big banger,' and in 1964, at the age of 20, he bought himself a 500cc Gold Star: a machine that would not only carry him to many wins, but also lead him to meet Mike Drayton, a man who would later play an important part in both his racing and business careers.

"At that time I was only about ten stone, so as I quickly discovered racing a 380lb Goldie was hard work, and it gave my body one hell of a pounding. I was friendly with one of our local farmers who allowed me to practice in one of his fields, and one day I met this chap – Mike Drayton – who turned up with an old Triumph scrambler. The Goldie's engine had lost its edge, but I was no mechanic and had no real idea what the problem was, so he asked me if I would like him to take a look at it. I could see he was a wizard with the spanners, and in no time at all he'd whipped the head off and discovered a burnt valve. With the engine back on song I had some decent results on the BSA, but it was around this time I first met Tim Pritchard, who loaned me a Westbury Metisse for a couple of meetings."

Tim's business at Westbury Hill was starting to take off, and what began as a few odd rides in the summer of '64 would, over the following years, lead to numerous other outings on Westbury-sponsored machines and also a lifelong friendship between the two. During the seasons of 1964-'66 Rob would ride not only the Westbury bikes, but also his own BSA and a Metisse owned by the Chilcott brothers; this which, as he told me, led to a whole new world of business for the young man from South Brewham.

"I rode three different Triumph Metisses, a BSA Victor, and also a Greeves Griffon – which I looped at Tweseldown and broke my collarbone – for Tim but it was all fairly informal, which meant I could also ride my own Goldie and I also had a few outings on a bottle green Metisse owned by the Chilcott brothers, who ran a small motorcycle shop in Shirehampton [Bristol]. They were two great enthusiasts, and although I only raced their bike a handful of times we immediately hit it off, and six months after first meeting them they asked me if I was interested in buying their motorcycle business. The offer was that they would let me have the lease for nothing and would sell me all of the stock – mostly Vespas and Mobylette mopeds – for £1500. I was still working in the family bakery – earning about £10 a week – so that sort of money seemed like a fortune, and I also needed to talk it through with my mother and father. They had always been two fantastic parents, and my father's response was that, as my brother and I would someday inherit the bakery and shop, he would give me £1000 towards getting the bike business up and running. It meant that I had to borrow the other £500, and I vividly recall going along to Bruton to see the bank manager Mr Burns, an ex-RAF man with a huge handlebar moustache and who always wore a tweed jacket. At that time I had no idea about running a business – I hardly knew what a cheque book looked like – but after reminding me I had to pay the money back Mr Burns agreed to the loan, and a few weeks later I was the owner of a motorcycle shop. Not only did I have a business, I also inherited Colin

the mechanic, who, thankfully for me, knew Vespa and Mobylette engines inside out."

Throughout the summer of 1966 Rob was not only running his newly acquired bike business, he was also racing every weekend, and typical headlines from the era read "Taylor supreme" and "Rob wins double" as the wins came thick and fast. Most of these came on his own 400cc Husqvarna, on which he competed in selected rounds of the British championship and also the big national meetings, but racing on the continent had to be put on hold, as back in Bristol there was a burgeoning business to run.

"It was a steep learning curve running a bike shop, but things were going well until the end of '66, when Colin – my mechanic – and his family decided to emigrate to Canada. My first reaction was to go and see Mike Drayton – the man who had worked wonders on my Goldie – and I asked him if he would like to come and work for me. His immediate answer was 'Yes,' and during the Christmas week of that year we shipped him, along with his wife and two small children, into the flat above the shop. Mike was a great guy, and we both worked tirelessly day and night building the business – which by then also included Puch – and when it became available I took over the old grocery shop next door to house the Puch bicycles. After a while we dropped Vespas, but by then I'd got to know Harold Fowler, and thanks to him we later got the Honda agency. With the full range of Japan's number one filling our floor space things really took, and I took on another mechanic to help Mike in the workshop, which was constantly busy preparing new bikes."

Away from the business, Rob and his brace of 250 and 360cc Huskys continued to notch up numerous wins, and this rich vein of form on the Swedish two-strokes led – via Harold Fowler – to another works ride, this time with AJS, on its new range of Stormer motocrossers.

"During the winter of 1968-'69 Harold Fowler approached me, and asked if I would be interested in riding a couple of sponsored 250 and 360cc AJSs for them in the new season. The deal was that they would supply the bikes – to be fettled by Mike – and all my spares, but at the time I don't think Harold had any idea of the amount we would get through, and at the end of that season he said to me 'I think you'd better join the factory team for next year.' The official works line-up consisted of me, Andy Roberton, and Malcolm Davis, and although we all had some good days the Ajays had niggling problems, and when my frame broke at a race in the south of France I decided enough was enough, and I reverted to a pair of Westbury Husqvarnas. When I returned the AJS to the factory, Peter Inchley asked me to take the Huskys along so he could take them for a spin on the test track at Thruxton; I remember he returned from his ride, got off the bike and said 'We can't compete with this.'"

Back on the ultra-reliable Swedish two-strokes Rob soon returned to his winning ways, although few could have expected his stunning ride in that year's British 500cc Grand Prix at Farleigh Castle. Cheered on by the huge crowd – and thousands more watching on TV – he finished runner-up in the first two 42-lap races, but by the end of the second leg the Husqvarna's clutch was on its last legs.

"Because I wasn't a regular in the world championship events there was no pressure on me, and it was one of those days when everything went absolutely perfectly. I had to ride most of the second leg with no clutch, but managed to finish, and between races I went to find the Husqvarna importer Brian Leask. I asked him if he could let me

Rob in forceful style on his way to victory on the Westbury Husky. He finished runner-up in the British motocross GP in 1970.

have a set of plates, but he returned from his van and gave me a whole new clutch unit, which Mike fitted in time for the third leg. By the end of the race I had no skin left on my hand, but I managed to finish eighth, which meant that I secured second overall behind Bengt Aberg and went home with £335 prize money in my pocket."

It was a fantastic day's sport, but, as he recalled, one in which he was lucky to finish.

"The following Wednesday I took the Huskys down to Sandy Bay to ride in one of their popular evening meetings, and after three laps in practice the 400 stopped dead. We got it back to the pits and discovered a small screw had fallen out of the points and jammed the flywheel; that's how close I came to not finishing the third leg of the GP."

The 250cc Husqvarna took Rob to a couple of wins that evening, but a few weeks later he received a call from Brian Leask, and two days after that he was bound for the USA.

"Out of the blue Brian called me and told me that Husqvarna were looking for another top rider to go to America to compete in the 250cc Inter-Am series, and would I like to? I only had two days to make up my mind, but my family and Mike all said 'Go,' so I packed my bag and a couple of days later found myself on a 747 bound for the USA. That said, the 747 never got farther than the runway when one of its engines blew up, and all the passengers had to get off and be transferred on to two other planes. Sadly, as I later discovered, I went on the one which landed in Chicago while my riding gear went on the other to Columbus, in Ohio. Along with the three Swedish riders – Kring, Aberg, and Christer Hammergren – I was met by the Husqvarna importer John Penton Snr, who supplied all our bikes and transport for the two-month race series, and a few days later we were off to the first meeting at Elkhorn in Wisconsin. In borrowed riding gear I had a fourth, fifth, and a big crash before the long drive to Pepperell in Massachusetts for the second round, where my flywheel key broke and I had to retire. Travelling all those miles in the van with the three Swedes was hard work, as they spent most of the time talking to each other in their native language, but after a meeting with the events organiser, Edison Dye, he teamed me up with state champion – and fellow Husky rider – Dick Robins. We immediately hit it off – we're still friends today – and for the next two months travelled all across the states covering thousands of miles. I had a few good rides with some thirds and fourths, but the hard desert tracks gave the bikes one hell of a hammering, and we were extremely thankful to the local Husqvarna agents who kept us topped up with spares and treated us like royalty along the way."

After two hard months, which included a broken bone in his foot after a pile-up in Tulsa, Rob was back home for another season on the Westbury-sponsored Huskys. However, Maicos was now making its mark in the UK, and, in 1972, Rob took up Badger Goss' offer to race a pair of the West German two-strokes.

"At first it seemed a bit strange lining up at the start alongside my 'boss,' but the Maicos were great bikes to ride, and during the four seasons I raced them they were both fast and extremely reliable. In addition to Mike I also had Malcolm Trevitt helping me out in the pits, and the bikes were always in tip-top condition – all I had to do was race them. During that first 1972 season I managed to finish third in the British 250cc championship, and I was also selected to ride in the Trophee des Nations team. This was at Ghent in Belgium, and I was third coming up though the woods, but missed a gear, and as a result I was struck on the arm by Heikki Mikola and flew over the railings. It was the end of my days racing and after a traumatic trip back to England – which saw my arm swell up like a balloon – I was out of action for the next six weeks. During the winter Mary Driver at the ACU asked me if I would like to contest the world 250 rounds but with a young family and a business to run I had to decline and other than my selection for the Motocross des Nations team in Sweden in 1974 – where we finished third – most of my racing was limited to that on home soil."

For those of us lucky enough to see him in action, there is little doubt that at his peak in the early '70s Rob was capable of taking on and beating the best in the world. But by 1976 he was past his best, and decided to call it a day.

"We then had three shops, and with younger riders coming through I decided at 32 it was time to pack it in, and I returned the Maicos back to Badger Goss. I announced in the press that I'd retired, but one morning I had a phone call from Don Howlett at Comerfords, who asked me if I would like to race a 250 and 360 KTM for them. I told him that I'd finished, but he persuaded me to go up to Thames Ditton to try them out, and the next thing I knew I was back racing in the British championship rounds."

Rob's new job as KTM test rider lasted for two years, and in-between filling out report forms for Don he showed he could still mix it with the best, securing some decent third and fourth places on the Austrian two-strokes. The 1978 season was his last in the cut and thrust of the British championships, but was not the end of the Rob Taylor racing career. He continued to race for two more years in the Haynes four-stroke series aboard a Curtis-framed XR 500 Honda, and, despite not riding in all of the rounds, he was still good enough to finish runner-up to Kenny Hanson in the '79 championships.

After 20 years of racing Rob finally decided to retire at the end of the 1980 season, bringing the curtain down on two memorable decades. The former baker's boy from South Brewham, still fondly remembered by a legion of West Country fans as one of the best scramblers of his generation.

Big thanks to Rob and Hazel for their time and hospitality, and for reliving some wonderful memories.

Full throttle on the Badger Goss-sponsored Maico.

"THE MAICOS WERE
GREAT BIKES TO
RIDE, AND DURING
THE FOUR SEASONS
I RACED THEM THEY
WERE BOTH FAST
AND EXTREMELY
RELIABLE"

Race action from Rob's last season on the
KTM.

A quiet and reserved West Country man, who was only 17 when he rode in his first British experts, and won the prestigious Pinhard trophy the same year. For 14 seasons Bill went up against and often beat the top talent in the competitive arena of one-day trials.

CHAPTER 12

BILL MARTIN – THE GOOD LIFE

"Giant-killer Bill Martin" was the *Motorcycling* headline after the 23-year-old Devonian had conquered rain, mud, rocks and raging water to win the gruelling Wye Valley Traders Cup trial in April 1960. On his works James, Martin was the only rider to master the long rock-filled gulley that formed the opening hazard at Hill Lane, and after surviving an impromptu dip into a stream he'd kept his composure to scoop the premier award by one solitary mark, ahead of the Tiger Cub ridden by Gordon Blakeway.

That Wye Valley victory – the first for the AMC-engined two-stroke – was a great one for the popular young man from Newton Abbot, who was undoubtedly one of the best trials riders of his generation over a glittering 14-year career, in which he would be awarded the prestigious Pinhard prize, qualify for the British experts, and earn a works bike for his skill and endeavours – all before he turned 18.

Well over 40 years have now passed since Bill hung up his Barbour jacket for the last time, but he still lives just a stone's throw from some of the sections he rode with such aplomb for perhaps his greatest triumph: winning the West of England *Motor Cycle* Cup in October 1958. A beautiful part of south Devon, where we met and

relieved some of those magical days when WH Martin and his factory James took on and beat the trials world's best.

Born in Bristol in June 1936, he was ten when his family moved to Buckfastleigh, in Devon, and it was here on a hot summer's day in 1951 that he got his first taste of off-road motorcycling.

"From our house in the Old Totnes Road I could hear a lot of noisy engines roaring away at nearby Wallaford Down, so I decided to cycle over to find out what was going on. On arrival I discovered it was the annual Patchquick trophy scramble, and by the end of the afternoon's racing I'd made my mind up that when I was old enough, I was going to have my own motorcycle. Of course in those days there was no such thing as schoolboy sport, and although he had no interest in motorcycling my father was soon enrolled into the idea of me taking to two wheels. A couple of months later he dropped me off in nearby Newton Abbot to have my hair cut, and afterwards I strolled around the corner to look at the bikes inside Greens motorcycle showroom. Imagine my surprise when I looked through the window and there was my dad talking to the salesman; he turned and saw me, and after beckoning me in his first words were 'What do you want then?'

"By the end of that afternoon I was the proud owner of a 125cc

Still only 17, his first ride in the British experts in 1953.

Works James team at the start of the Scottish Six Days in 1954.

Francis Barnett Merlin, but I was still only 15 so for the best part of nine months, my riding was restricted to the paddock and orchard at the rear of our house. At that time I had little or no idea what a trial was, but having to negotiate the muddy tracks with a ribbed front tyre was hard going, and I got pretty good at riding feet-up on the little Barnett. A week after my 16th birthday in June 1952 I rode in my first event: an Otter vale novice trial, in which I finished third."

Bill's debut ride was aboard a pukka 197cc trial's Franny Barnett – a 16th birthday present from his parents – which he took to like a duck to water, and by the middle of the following month he won his first novice cup. This was quickly followed by a non-expert award and barely three months after he'd started riding he was upgraded to an expert. By the beginning of October he was competing in his first national and impressing some established stars, although as he recalled at the time he had no idea of who they were.

"I'd entered our local national – the West of England – and on the Friday before the trial my local dealer, Freddie Hawken, asked me if I would like to go out practising with him. About 20 of us met up at his shop in Newton Abbot, although I didn't have a clue who any of the others were. We went to Gatcombe and then on to Harper's hill near Totnes, and all I knew was that two of them were named 'Jeff' – I later learnt that they were Jeff Smith and Geoff Duke – and there was another who parked his bike against a tree and smoked his pipe while closely watching me ride the Barnett up and down the muddy banks."

What Bill didn't realise at the time was that the man was AMC ace and competition chief Hugh Viney, who was left extremely impressed

by the L-plated youngster on the little two-stroke. At close quarters Viney could see the teenager's huge potential, which in the following day's trial earned him a first class award, and, 12 months later, the prestigious Pinhard trophy and a ride on the works James.

The Pinhard was awarded annually by the Sunbeam MCC to the young rider under 21 adjudged to have made the most meritorious achievement in motorcycle sport, and after a wonderful first season – in which he qualified for the British experts – few could disagree with the winner for 1953.

"After the West of England I started doing quite a few of the nationals, but I was still only 16 so I didn't have a car or van, so my bike and I were taken by one of our local star riders, Eddie Hayne or 'Nipper' Parsons. This was all arranged by my father, who – although he had no interest in motorcycling himself – was very supportive of my trials riding career. I won two class awards in nationals during the 1952-'53 season, which meant that, aged 17, I qualified for the British experts; I think that at the time I might have been the youngest ever rider. As a result, the West of England 'chairman' – and former top lady trials rider – Mrs Miriam Anning put my name forward for the Pinhard prize, and I was over the moon when I received the letter from the ACU to say that I'd won it. The trophy was presented to me by Graham Walker at the '53 motorcycle show at Earls Court, and standing on the edge of the stage was the same man who I'd seen at Harper's Lane: Hugh Viney. At the end of the presentation he approached me and asked if I would be interested in riding a works James. As you can imagine, it didn't take long for me to give my answer. The week after

Wilf Hadon, Des May, and Mr Leigh watch the action at the Rock 'n' Roll section in the Tiverton trial in 1958.

Off-Road Giants!

Christmas I drove up to Plumpstead – I now had my own Ford Thames van – and spent a week going through all the production stages at the factory and practising on my brand new J9 James. Much of this was either at Brands Hatch or at Gordon Jackson's farm, but, on returning to Plumpstead, my first job was to clean both of the bikes. Hugh would leave me to wash them down, and when I'd finished I had to ring the bell and he would come and inspect every nook and cranny to make sure they were to his requirements. He was a real stickler for presentation, and one of the first lessons he taught me was that trials were won in the workshop, and, as a works rider, I was at all times representing the factory. He was of course an outstandingly good rider, and he certainly taught me a lot on how best to negotiate the slippery stuff up at Jackson's farm. I think by the end of that wonderful week he had turned me from a good amateur into a decent professional. He helped me a lot, and I had a great deal of respect for him."

It only took a week for Bill to put Viney's tuition into practice, with an outstanding ride in the St David's trade-supported trial at Neath, where he won the 200cc cup on the rigid-framed J9 James. He followed this a few weeks later with another class cup in a muddy Cotswold. By May, Martin and his fellow team members, Brian Povey and Peter Stirland, were in the Highlands for the annual six days trial, and the man from Devon was soon on the leader board. For a few hours on the fourth day he was briefly in the lead, but sadly a dream debut victory was ruled out by a crash on the Thursday, which, as he told me, left him with a nasty injury.

"In the week before the Scottish, Brian, Peter, and I had ridden in the Travers trial, and then spent several days practicing in the Highlands before the weigh-in on Sunday. I think the first day's run was something like 184 miles – a long way on a little two-stroke – but if I had any doubt about the route I just 'followed my nose' and tuned in to the smell of the burning oil from Jimmy Alves' Triumph Terrier. I loved the rocks, and I'd discovered that by using a lot of back brake – while still allowing the motor to pull against it – I could ride with no chain snatch, which meant that the bike rarely broke traction. This was perfect for negotiating both rocks and slippery adverse cambers, but as a result I was getting through two pairs of brake shoes a day. I was doing okay, but on the fourth day I crashed avoiding a car on a narrow track and the bike landed on top of me in the ditch. Thankfully two other competitors stopped and dragged both me and the bike out onto the tarmac, but I'd badly twisted my knee, and I was in agony as I rode on to the lunch stop. This was at an old army camp, where we managed to find a couple of bed slats, which were taped around my leg to form a splint. As you can imagine, it was okay pushing the gear lever down, but impossible to pull it up, so I rigged up a length of string between the petrol cap and the gear lever. It worked okay and at least I managed to finish the trial."

That Bill managed to ride the last two days, *and* win a first class award with what was later discovered to be a broken kneecap speaks volumes for his tenacity; a trait that he had precious little time to demonstrate when, in September of 1954, he made his ISDT debut in Wales. Unfortunately his international career proved to be an extremely short one, as on day one he was involved in a head-on collision with a Czech competitor who had gone the wrong way. With the works James badly damaged – and the same knee injured again – he was an early retirement. He also tried his hand at scrambling, but, after being run over and badly bruised, decided that he lacked the all

important aggression to be a successful racer, so speed events were not for him.

On the work front, Bill had gone to work for ex-TT and scrambles star Freddie Hawken as an apprentice mechanic. This conveniently kept him out of doing national service, meaning his trials career continued unhindered. There were countless wins in local club and open to centre events, first class awards, and class cups in many nationals – including the '55 Scottish – on the 197cc James; the same machine that carried him to his first national premier award in that year's John Douglas in north Somerset. An unusually dry event, which, as Bill recalled, was ideally suited to his little two-stroke.

"The John Douglas had a reputation for thick black mud and slippery rocks, but, after several weeks without rain, sections like the first one at Cowsh were bone dry, and the organisers had to resort to using lots of tape. The net result was plenty of tight 'nadgery' sections, which were perfect for my rear brake riding style, and in a great days sport I only lost two marks all day."

Three years would elapse before Bill won his next national, but in-between there were plenty of class wins, a change of machine, and a frustrating year on the sidelines before he bounced back with perhaps his best ever season in 1958.

"The J9 was a good bike but I fancied a go on a 'big 'un' like Gordon Jackson's, so after talking to Hugh Viney he arranged for me to have a 350cc Matchless for the '56 season. It was a lovely bike, and although I managed to win a few open to centre events, I wasn't as successful on it as the James two-stroke, and after 12 months I gave it back to the factory. I was having a lot of trouble with my knee – the one which had been injured in the Scottish and again in that head-on in the ISDT – so it meant an operation, and I missed the whole of the 1957 season. I could easily have called it a day, but in January 1958 I went to the West of England dinner/dance and got talking to the James competition chief Bob Bicknell, who said 'Want another go then Bill?' Answering that I did, he said 'I'll send one down on the train for you next week.' True to his word the bike – a works 201cc James TOE 431 – turned up at Newton Abbot railway station early on the following Sunday morning, and after fuelling it up, I rode it down to the White Hart pub in Buckfastleigh for the start for the local Knill trial, which was regarded as a 'mini' West of England."

Bill had been out of action for 12 months, and he was on an untried bike, but it was soon apparent he'd lost none of his old skill, and at the end of a tough day's sport he ran out comfortable winner ahead of the best of the south western centre stars. He was back with a bang, and in the following months won no fewer than eight successive club and open to centre events on the trot. Hundreds of miles were covered competing in important nationals, although it was fitting that his biggest win in '58 came very close to home, with the West of England Silver Jubilee trial: an event that, as he recalled, tested both the organising club and all of the riders to the extreme.

"Throughout Friday rain had lashed down in torrents, and it was still pouring down when we lined up for the start on Saturday morning. As a result of flooding, four sections were cancelled, but clerk of the course Richard Walford and his team had done a fantastic job marking out the route, and, despite the weather, it was a terrific trial. By the finish we were all soaking wet, but for me everything had gone perfectly, and when the results were announced I discovered I'd beaten Peter Stirland by just one mark to take the premier."

West of England, October 1959. Bill goes clean at Upper Diamond Lane.

Bill pops a wheelie on the 250 James, on his way to special first class in the SSDT, 1962. (Courtesy Gordon Francis)

"BILL HAD BEEN OUT
OF ACTION FOR 12
MONTHS, AND HE
WAS ON AN UNTRIED
BIKE, BUT IT WAS
SOON APPARENT HE'D
LOST NONE OF HIS
OLD SKILL"

The rest of the winter of 1958 saw the James star travelling the length and breadth of the country, but, thanks to some 'lateral thinking,' there were always some clean clothes and hot water to greet him at the end of a gruelling event. The legendary Scott time and observation trial also left him extremely fatigued, as he revealed.

"I always carried spare clothes with me, and made a point of wrapping them up around two hot water bottles, this meant that at the end of a cold trial I had some nice warm clothes to put on, and also hot water to wash my hands and face. Other than that one day in the '54 ISDT and the odd scramble I'd steered clear of speed events, but for some reason in the winter of 1958 I decided to give the Scott time and observation trial a go. I managed to get round, but I was absolutely exhausted. After the event I had to drive down to London to be on the James stand at the motorcycle show, and I don't think I could stand properly for about three days."

After missing the '58 Scottish Bill was back in the Highlands for the 1959 trial, but by now the 201cc James had been pensioned off, and he was on the new AMC-engined factory machine. It was now a full 250, but one that, as he told me, gave a very different power delivery to the old 197cc Villiers engine he was accustomed to.

"I used the 201cc bike for the winter of '58-'59, but as the factory were now using a 250cc Piatti engine in their road bikes they decided to use the same motor in the new trials machine. The first time I saw it was when it arrived on the train from the factory in Birmingham and after running it in I disassembled it and squeezed it into the back of my car before heading off to Scotland. On arrival in Edinburgh the comp shop boys were thrown into a panic because at first they couldn't work out where my bike was, and when they discovered my James 'flat pack' they threw serious doubt into my ability to reassemble it in time for the Sunday weigh-in. I'm happy to say I managed it, but as the trial progressed I had to alter my riding style to get the best from the AMC engine. There was plenty of top-end, but little in the way of torque, so the only way to ride it was to keep the engine buzzing and scream it in first gear. In fact I had quite a good ride, and after most of the works BSAs had dropped out with various electrical and mechanical problems I won the 250cc cup that year."

Over the next two seasons Bill continued to develop and improve the 250cc James, and despite the engine's buzzy nature he notched up some impressive wins, among them that memorable one at the wet Wye Valley in April 1960, which, 50 years on, he recalled with a wry smile.

"From early morning it was pouring down with rain, and as the trial got under way we had to negotiate streams which had turned into frightening torrents. Crossing one of these I dropped the bike and was soaked from head to toe. Wet and cold I struggled on, but had a spate of punctures – four in total – and with the tyre flat I managed to limp to a garage where I carried out some hasty repairs. With it mended and re-inflated I seriously considered retiring, but on arrival at the next section – and yet another puncture – I was told by the observer that due to the weather the final group had been cancelled, and this would be the last one. I was so fed up I didn't even walk the section, and attacked it flat out in second gear. Much to my surprise I went clean, and was told by the observer it was the first feet-up climb of the day. I got to the finish and was all for loading up and heading for home, until an official approached me and asked if I wanted to sign off. I scribbled my name, and when the results arrived a couple of days later I was glad that I had, because much to my surprise I'd won the premier award by one mark

from Gordon Blakeway. The following week's *Motor Cycling* had the headline 'Giant-Killer Bill Martin,' but they had no idea of just how close I'd come to throwing the towel in.

"I think I'm correct in saying it was the first and last trade-supported trials win for the Piatti-engined bike. I persevered with it for two seasons and had some good rides in both open to centre and national events before the factory decided to revert back to a 32A Villiers motor in 1962, and my new bike, 284 FON, duly turned up on the train. Living so far from Birmingham I had little direct contact with the factory, so it was very much a case of them supplying me with a free bike, and I was left to maintain and ride it. They in turn sorted out and paid for all of my entries, and also covered my expenses for competing in major events. I only rode 284 FON for one season, and was then told that the James trials team was being disbanded so the comp shop could concentrate their efforts on scrambles, and all of the works riders were being transferred to Francis Barnett's."

Fitted with its 32A Villiers engine and Marcelle square barrel, the works Franny B turned out to be quite a useful tool, but, despite Bill's best efforts, it failed to last the distance in the '63 Scottish, and he was forced to retire on the final day.

"The gearbox broke on the Tuesday, but I managed to bodge it up and then had the choice of either first or third, which meant it was first for all the sections and flat out in third on the road. I managed to reach the overnight stop, but then had to leave it in the park ferme until the Wednesday morning, where, in the permitted 15 minutes before restart, I managed to change the complete gear cluster and selectors. I nursed it for the next three days, but on the Saturday it developed a serious 'death rattle' and seized near Glen Ogle.

"I was determined to finish, and when I saw a bike on a trailer managed to persuade a retiree to let me have his barrel and piston – I'm glad to report that the factory sent him new parts for his help – but sadly I only got as far as Stirling and the crankshaft broke. That was the end of my Scottish, and at the finish I was met by Hugh Viney, who smiled and said 'Well, at least you tried.'"

The '63 Highland classic would be Bill's last trip to Scotland – an event he reflects on as being his favourite in the trials calendar – and at the end of the year the works Barnett was returned to the factory.

"After chasing round the country riding in all the major trials for ten years I felt I was past my best, and decided to retire from the nationals and concentrate on events in my home south western centre. My works Barnett went back to the factory, and it was replaced by a semi-works Greeves supplied through Freddie Hawkens, who was their agent in south Devon. It was great in a straight line, and I had a few decent results on it, but I didn't like the handling characteristics of the leading link forks, and at the end of the 1965 season decided it was time to call it a day."

Later in 1970 Bill rode a 250cc Bultaco for a season "just for fun," and in the early '80s did a few pre-1965 events on his old James, but the end of that '65 season was effectively the date the curtain fell on his trials career. Fourteen magnificent seasons, in which the quiet lad from south Devon took on and beat the trials world's best, summed up by the man himself as "a good life."

Big thanks to Bill – now president of the West of England club – and his wife, Jean, for their time and hospitality, and to Dave Cole for his help and enthusiasm with this profile.

Bill on the 250 James in the 1962 south western inter-club team trial.
(Courtesy Gordon Francis)

Towards the end of his career, on the 250cc Greeves in 1964.

"I WAS SO FED UP I
DIDN'T EVEN WALK THE
SECTION, AND ATTACKED
IT FLAT OUT IN SECOND
GEAR. MUCH TO MY
SURPRISE I WENT CLEAN"

After riding a gutless BSA Bantam to victory in his first trial, Gordon went on to become one of the UK's leading all-rounders, and in 14 seasons there were few one-day trials, national scrambles, or international six-day events where his name didn't feature in the results.

CHAPTER 13

GORDON BLAKEWAY – A GREAT ALL-ROUNDER

Born in Stockton-on-Tees in 1935, Gordon Blakeway was one of that rare breed of true motorcycling all-rounders; a man equally at home keeping his feet firmly on the pegs while cleaning a tricky section in the Scottish Highlands, winning gold medals in the international six-day trial, or riding to victory at a championship scramble. By nature a self-effacing and modest man, the former Ariel, Triumph and AMC works rider is not one to brag about his achievements, but just a glance at any results in the long-faded pages of the Blue 'un or Green 'un between 1952 and the end of '66 will see the name 'Blakeway' sharing column space and accolades with his rivals and team-mates Sammy Miller, Ron Langston, Ken Heanes, John Giles, and Roy Peplow. In the history of off-road sport, there can be few competitors who won their first trial and even fewer who managed to land a works scrambler before they had ridden in a race, but back in the '50s it all happened to the young Yorkshireman; a lad who was born with motorcycling in his blood. Gordon takes up the story ...

"My dad was a founder member of the Stockton-on-Tees club and competed in all of the local trials, so from an early age bikes were part of my life. On reaching 16 I bought myself a secondhand 125cc BSA Bantam, which I rode to compete in the Stockton club's Linfoot Cup

trial for my first competitive event. I can remember that the Bantam was absolutely gutless and wouldn't pull your hat off, but my dad kept encouraging me to keep moving, and when the results appeared I was amazed to see I'd won the novice award."

To show that his win was no fluke, a month later Gordon competed in the Weardale trial, which he won outright. Still on the gallant little BSA, in March 1952 he sampled his first national – the Travers – but was excluded for finishing outside the time allowance in this super tough event. With a change to a more competitive 197cc James, Blakeway began the '53 season in fine style, pipping Gordon McLaughlan for the premier award in the Middlesbrough winter trial, and later that year he finished a creditable 18th out of only 29 finishers in one of the trials world's most arduous events; the Scott time and observation trial. Keen to expand his riding horizons, May '54 saw the youngster make his debut in the Scottish Highlands, but, after a promising start, he was forced to retire when the little two-stroke developed gearbox problems.

In major trials the big four-strokes still ruled the roost, and by the end of the '54-'55 season Gordon had abandoned the lightweight James in favour of a 500cc BSA Gold Star. It didn't take him long

The Ariel team of Sammy Miller, Gordon Blakeway, and Ron Langston, which won eight team prizes for the factory during 1958.

"MY DAD KEPT ENCOURAGING ME TO KEEP MOVING, AND WHEN THE RESULTS APPEARED I WAS AMAZED TO SEE I'D WON THE NOVICE AWARD"

Finding some grip in a muddy gully during the 1958 ISDT at Garmisch-Partenkirchen.

Flat out on the Triumph at the British motocross GP at Hawkstone Park, July 1962.

to adapt his riding style to the heavy Goldie, and on this machine he notched his first major win when representing Yorkshire in the 1956 inter-centre team trial, where he achieved best individual performance. His impressive victory certainly caught the eye of one of the sporting motorcycle world's great talent spotters – Ralph Venables – and for the '57 season he was signed to ride a works Ariel HT Single alongside Ron Langston and the Ulsterman Sammy Miller. He takes up the story again.

"Ariel's 'old guard' of Bob Ray and David Tye had decided to call it a day, and thanks to a recommendation from Ralph Venables – he knew all of the important and influential people in the British industry – I was approached by Ernie Smith and invited to join their works trials team."

Needless to say, it didn't take long for him to make up his mind, and he was allocated the factory HT 500 with number plate GOV 131. With Langston on 130 and Miller on the now legendary GOV 132, Ariel carried all before them, and in '58 was virtually invincible, winning no fewer that eight team prizes in the important trade-supported trials. Several of these featured the name of G S Blakeway with the premier award, and the same year he also finished fourth in the Scottish Six Days. Although Gordon had been signed to ride the works bike in one- and six-day trials, it didn't take him long to show his talent at speed events, and, in only his second season scrambling, he grabbed the local centre's motocross championship, and won the first of his four ISDT gold medals in the mud at Garmisch Partenkirchen. Some wonderful days, remembered with great fondness by the former Ariel star.

"Sammy Miller was then working at Selly Oak, and he was given pretty much free reign in developing his own bike, but those ridden by Ron and myself were standard HT 500s as sold to the public. When I signed on as a works rider they paid me a £50 retainer – this was good money in 1957 – and on top of that I received all of my travelling

expenses, plus bonuses from the plug and chain companies, and with Ariel sorting out all of the entries all I had to do was turn up and ride. Before and after a major event the bikes went back to the comp shop, where they were fettled and tuned by Seff Ellis (Scott's dad), although for the ISDT they were machines taken off the production line and – with the addition of a sportier cam from the scrambler – they were prepared for the tough six-day trial. Before that first international I'd been riding in scrambles during the summer – I'd had a good season and won the Yorkshire motocross championship on the HS – so I was feeling pretty fit, but as the ISDT was such an important event we'd had strict instructions from Ernie Smith to 'go careful and not to get injured.' As you can imagine, when I arrived to pick up my team-mate Ron for the trip to Germany, I was extremely surprised when he told me 'I've got a little scramble to ride in first.' He rode in two races – injury free – and we then drove off to the international, where he won his gold medal. I don't think Ernie ever got to know about him racing in the scramble."

The power delivery of the HT Ariel was ideally suited to the slippery rocks found in the Wye Valley national trial, and it proved to be one of Gordon's favourites as he scooped the premier award three years on the trot. However, by the end of '59 the ailing Selly Oak factory abandoned the manufacture of its competition machines in order to concentrate on the Ariel Leader, and the new decade saw the Yorkshire market-gardener mounted on a 199cc Triumph Tiger Cub. He took to the little Cub like a duck to water, and for the next three seasons there were scores of important trials where Blakeway and the little Triumph featured in the results. Not just in the UK – by now he was spreading his wings to the continent, and a typical weekend in November 1960 saw him finish runner-up to fellow Yorkshireman Bill Wilkinson in the British experts on the Saturday, before loading up and heading off to France where he won the tough international St Cucufa trial near Paris on the Sunday. The Cub was also ideally suited to the rocks in the Scottish Six Days and after finishing a close fourth in '61 he looked to be going one place higher the following year. But, after six hard days battling with Miller and Gordon Jackson, the Triumph man was thwarted when the distributor seized a mere ten miles from the finish, leaving the hapless rider kicking his heels at the roadside. At the start of his career as a works Triumph trials rider he was still scrambling his old Selly Oak single, and, although there had been no development to the big four-stroke with Blakeway in the saddle, it was still seriously competitive. After some stunning performances in his home centre he was appointed captain for the 1960 north versus south scramble, and justified that honour by being top scorer on the big Ariel. This in turn prompted Henry Vale to supply him with one of the works 500cc scramblers, as raced so successfully by John Giles, Roy Peplow, and Ken Heanes. As he recalled, this led to some successful and memorable trips to the continent.

"Living in the north of England meant that just getting to Dover to catch the ferry was a trip of around 300 miles – a long day's drive in the pre-motorway days – before the onward journey through France, Holland or Belgium. I covered countless thousands of miles in my Morris Oxford pick-up – often in the company of my pal and fellow rider Peter Fletcher – but it was all worth it, as the crowds were very enthusiastic, and the continental organisers paid us some decent start and prize money to cover the costs. During the three years I raced the Triumph I registered a few wins at non-international meetings in

Trying hard on the ex-Gordon Jackson AJS on the Scottish rocks.

"AS THE ISDT WAS SUCH AN IMPORTANT EVENT WE'D HAD STRICT INSTRUCTIONS FROM ERNIE SMITH TO 'GO CAREFUL AND NOT TO GET INJURED'"

Gordon finding plenty of grip on the works AMC single in the 1963 Welsh three day trial.

France, but my best result in a world championship round was when I finished fourth behind Bill Nillson and Sten Lundin in Germany, and I also clocked a highly satisfying fifth in the British round at Hawkstone Park in '62."

The combination of skills Gordon had honed competing in both trials and scrambles were ideally suited to the long distance endurance speed events like the Welsh – which he won two years on the trot – the three-day Tatra in Poland, and the ISDT. The strength-sapping international (the motorcycling world's 'Olympics') became one of his all time favourites, and the event centred on Llandrindod Wells in 1961 saw the works Triumph man at his scintillating best. As a member of the Silver Vase team he powered the 500cc twin to a glorious gold medal-winning ride through the Welsh mud, and in doing so accumulated the highest amount of bonus points obtained by any British competitor. Triumph was quick to capitalise on his stunning ride with several full page adverts in the weekly Blue 'un and Green 'un, but, 12 months later, as a member of the British Trophy team, a poorly prepared, uncompetitive machine led to retirement in West Germany.

"It was Triumph's policy to allocate bikes of 350, 500 and 650cc to all of its works riders for the six days, and for the '63 trial in Garmisch I was allocated the smallest of the twins. As I'd discovered in the Welsh three-day, the little 350 had to be ridden virtually flat out to keep to a gold medal time schedule, but the engine in the bike for the international was absolutely gutless; the overall gearing was too high and after nursing it for five days I eventually had to retire on the last day when the clutch burnt out. Needless to say I was less than pleased to be supplied with a sub-standard machine, and after a harsh exchange of words with Henry Vale it led to the end of my days as a works rider with Triumph."

However, as one door closed another quickly opened for the talented Yorkshire all-rounder, and for the '62-'63 winter season he found himself the new member of the AMC factory team.

"Gordon Jackson had decided to retire at the end of '62, so I was approached by Hugh Viney and asked to take over the vacant place in the factory team on the AJS – 187 BLF – on which he (Jackson) had won the Scottish with his famous 'one dab' victory in 1961. Jacko loved the power characteristics of the short stroke motor, but Mr Viney figured that the longer stroke one would probably suit me better, so before my first competitive ride the bike was treated to an engine transplant. It was certainly very different to the lightweight Tiger Cub I'd been riding for the last three years, but I eventually got to grips with it and registered my first win in a Yorkshire open to centre event. A couple of weeks later I competed in the National St David's trial near Neath, and when the provisional results were announced many of the top runners had been excluded for being out of the time allowance, and I was awarded the premier award. Because it was a championship event the exclusions promoted a lot of protests, and, some weeks later when the amended results appeared, I'd lost the premier and had to be content with a first class award."

Due to the thick blanket of snow and ice that covered much of the UK, many trials were cancelled in the early months of '63, but by May things were back to normal, and it was time for the annual trip to Scotland. Gordon ran in the top ten all week on the bike that had won the event two years earlier, but although he was never in a position to challenge winner Arthur Lampkin on the factory BSA, he finished a strong eighth, and, along with Mick Andrews and Gordon McLaughlin, was part of the AJS trio that scooped the prestigious team award that year.

After a season scrambling the works 500cc Matchless – not remembered as his most favourite machine – autumn saw the Yorkshire all-rounder off on his travels behind the Iron Curtain, but, as he recalled, both the Tatra in Poland and the international six days in Czechoslovakia ended in frustrating retirements on the factory Ajay.

"For those of us who had been brought up in the West, travelling into and through the Soviet-controlled countries in Eastern Europe was a real eye-opener. As we quickly discovered, all of the media was controlled by the state, and the average person had little idea of what was going on in the world outside the Eastern bloc. Nearly all of the buildings were grey, and although the people were keen to talk to us and find out a little about our lives they told us that every move was monitored, and police informers were everywhere. The Tatra trial itself was extremely well organised, with soldiers at all of the road junctions making sure we didn't deviate off the route, but it was also extremely hard going, and on the second day my AJS developed engine problems; I managed to limp on to the next time check but I was out of the event. At the control I discovered that Cliff Clayton had bent the front forks of his Ajay in a spill, so I agreed to ride on ahead, and when he came along we would change his for mine. This all went to plan until a battalion of Russian soldiers came marching down the track, so to avoid them seeing me I hastily covered up the bike with bracken and lay down in a ditch and waited for them to pass by. After they'd gone Cliff duly arrived, and after a lot of pulling and tugging we managed to remove his bent fork, stems, and with mine in place he was eventually on his way again. At the end of three hard days Sammy Miller was announced as winner, and along with a huge three-foot high glass trophy he was presented with a new Polish motorcycle, which he kicked into life and with the aid of a huge 'dab' he rode off the stage."

With the engine gremlins sorted, Gordon and the same AJS were chosen to represent the British Trophy team for the '63 ISDT in Czechoslovakia; the long trip now well remembered for the infamous transport breakdown, and the skill and improvisation shown in eventually getting to the start and back home again from the super tough event.

"It was decided that some of the Trophy and Vase team riders, along with their bikes, would be taken in a BSA lorry driven by John Harris and Jim Sandiford, while the rest of the riders would make it there under their own steam in cars. The truck – which was normally used for dropping off bikes to dealers around the Midlands –got as far as the autobahn in West Germany when it developed a horrible noise from the engine, and we ground to a halt with a blown big end. We were still miles from the Czech border, and as all the bikes were on the lorry there was no other alternative than to try to carry out some sort of repair. Johnny Giles and Scott Ellis got the sump off in a lay-by, while Henry Vale went off to Frankfurt to source some new big end shells. We cleaned up the big end journal the best we could and reassembled the engine, but it only did another 20 miles or so before it went bang again. Gilo decided that the only course of action was to take the piston and con rod out and run the engine on five cylinders, so we spent a whole day stripping and reassembling it with a piece of leather belt strapped around the big end journal. We started it up and it sounded terrible, but at least it ran and we struggled along. After a long delay

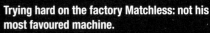

"A BATTALION OF RUSSIAN SOLDIERS CAME MARCHING DOWN THE TRACK, SO TO AVOID THEM SEEING ME I HASTILY COVERED UP THE BIKE WITH BRACKEN AND LAY DOWN IN A DITCH"

Clocking in behind a CZ rider during the '64 ISDT in East Germany, where he won a gold medal on the AMC factory single.

we managed to get through the Czech border control, and, covered in muck and oil, eventually arrived at the trials headquarters late on the Saturday afternoon."

With every checkpoint linked to the start by radio, and scores of first aid teams dotted around the course, the Czech organisation was second to none. However, due to heavy rain it was hard going for the 280 riders, and Sammy Miller was quoted at the time saying 'that parts of the course would do justice to a national one-day trial.' Period reports paint a vivid picture of wet and exhausted riders trying to negotiate slippery rocks, and of numerous retirements due the transmission and gearbox failures. After their heroic efforts the previous year, the British Trophy team members were optimistic they would be able to challenge the East Germans on their quick and ultra reliable MZs, but sadly their hopes were dashed early on day one. First they lost John Harris when his oil pump packed up, and the BSA man was soon joined by the unlucky Blakeway, when the lower eye of his bike's rear suspension snapped off after being struck by a broken brake anchorage arm. At the end of six hard days the East Germans narrowly beat the Guzzi-mounted Italians to scoop the international trophy; a win that meant that, 12 months later, it was another trip behind the Iron Curtain.

Based at Erfurt in the forested mountains of the Thuringa Wald, the event was the first and only international run in East Germany, and one now famous for the first appearance of two American Vase teams – one including Hollywood legend Steve McQueen – mounted on 500 and 650cc Triumph twins. The trial itself is on record in the period press as being 'too easy,' 'boring,' and 'monotonous,' but it was events away from the motorcycling that left a lasting impression on the AJS man.

"The road trip from the UK was trouble-free, but our arrival at the border coincided with that of the American team, and it took ages while the guards checked with their superiors in Berlin to see if it was okay to let them in, and if McQueen had made any anti-communist films. Every car, van and pick-up was thoroughly examined inside and out by sombre and sour-faced guards, but after several hours we were eventually given permission to enter with strict instructions not to stop or to take any photos in the heavily fortified 'no-man's land.' The difference after driving through West Germany was quite staggering, as other than army wagons there was virtually no traffic, and most of the roads had a green strip of grass growing down the middle. Many of the houses were brightly painted, but we later leaned that this had been a communist ploy to give the impression of affluence to the Western visitors, while away from this facade we soon discovered that, although everyone had a job, there was little in the shops, and all lived in fear of the secret police.

"The organisers had brought in some fruit for the competitors, but the standard of the food we were supplied with was pretty awful. When we complained and asked for some good old bacon and eggs, we were told that they had calculated the calories we would burn each day and the food was sufficient for our needs. Some of the fruit had previously never been seen in the East, and when Olga Kevelos offered a child a banana they had no idea how to peel it; needless to say, she was immediately pounced on by a policeman and given a stern lecture, and told that offering fruit to children was forbidden. We had little contact with the ordinary people, but spent many hours with the Americans drinking tea supplied by the Reynold chain rep Vic Doyle and his wife. These gatherings not only enabled us to relax and compare notes, but to listen to many of the hilarious stories which Steve McQueen had to tell about his experiences on the film sets and racing his bikes in the California deserts."

Racing in the mud was something new to most of the American riders, but they acquitted themselves well, and, despite losing both McQueen and their captain Bud Ekins after heavy crashes, both Cliff Coleman and Dave Ekins won gold and the team's reserve John Steen a silver on their big Triumph twins. Blakeway's 350cc AJS was unable to match the speed of the two-stroke MZs, but, despite heavy rain and thick fog on Tuesday's special test hillclimb, the AMC single performed faultlessly, and at the end of a hard week his total of just over 604 points was enough to secure yet another gold medal. It was a glorious international for the British Trophy team, as all five riders won gold and finished equal first with the host country, but were sadly beaten into second place by virtue of earning fewer bonus points than the East Germans. It was a performance that saw the following year's ISDT held in the Isle of Man, but there would be no Gordon Blakeway in the line up for the 1965 'motorcycling Olympics.'

"On leaving school I'd joined my parents in their market garden business, and they had always been hugely supportive of my competition career. There was never any problem in me taking time off work to compete in the Scottish and international six-day trial, or for long weekends when I needed to travel to the continent for an important scramble. I'd had some fantastic years on the bikes, but by the mid '60s I decided it was time to concentrate more on the business, so '64 was the last time I rode in Scotland and the ISDT. I continued to compete in national trials on 187 BLF, and I also rode a 250 James for a while, but it was obvious that AMC was in serious decline, and it came as little surprise when I was told that the competition department was being closed. I was keen to buy my famous Scottish winning AJS, so we agreed a price of £100, and as they owed me £65 in outstanding expenses it only actually cost me £35! During the following winter I had a few rides on one of the first production Bultacos and managed a decent third behind Sammy Miller and Don Smith in the St Cucafa European championship round, but an old scrambles injury necessitated the removal of a cartilage and I decided it was time to call it a day."

It brought the curtain down on 14 glorious years; but the name of Gordon Blakeway will be forever inscribed in the annals of motorcycle sport – not just as a brilliantly successful competitor, but, for all who met him, as a true gentleman.

With his tongue stuck out, Gordon takes a dab on the factory James in 1965.

A young Les with his first scrambles bike.

CHAPTER 14

LES ARCHER - DESTINY'S CHILD

The son of TT winner the 'Aldershot flyer,' it was no small wonder that Les Archer should become a motorcycle racer. From humble beginnings on a 350cc Matchless, he went on to become one of the leading scramblers of his generation.

It was a raw spring morning in early 1946, when a 16-year-old schoolboy turned up at Elvetham Park in Hampshire to ride in his first scramble. Aboard an ex-WD 350cc Matchless it was a tough race baptism, but the young man showed potential, and at the end of a muddy day's sport he proudly returned to his Petersfield home with a trophy – best performance of a rider aged under 20 years of age – for his endeavours.

The youngsters name was Les Archer; a man who, in the next decade, would take on and beat the cream of the motocross world on his Manx Norton-engined special. One of motorcycle racing's true greats, who rode for 20 memorable years, motoring thousands of miles across the near continent, earning a living and chasing championship points on his booming four-stroke single.

Over 40 years have now passed since the former 500cc European champion hung up his racing leathers, and he now lives in southern Spain with his wife, Claire. It was here I met with him to relive some of those halcyon days of motorcycle sport, and he began by telling me about the motorcycle dynasty – Archers of Aldershot – he was born into.

"My grandfather Jim – JC – left school in Andover when he was only aged 11, and got a job making hand-made bicycles. He was naturally gifted at making and repairing things, and soon progressed to a position as an apprentice motor mechanic in Aldershot. Later he started his own business selling and repairing cars, but it wasn't until well after the First World War he got into motorcycles. That was after my dad, LJ (Leslie James), had come top of the form at his school, and his reward was a Cedos two-stroke motorbike. He (LJ) quickly developed a passion for two wheels, so granddad decided to take on the Ner-a-Car agency, one of which dad rode in the MCC's Exeter and Land's End long-distance trials. Bitten by the competition bug, he fancied galloping the Ner-a-Car around Brooklands in one of their high-speed reliability trials, but, unfortunately, a week before the event he bent the bike competing in a scramble. Quite how he managed to get it we shall probably never know, but instead of the Ner-a-Car he came to the start line on a real racing New Imperial lent to him by the factory. He took to the New Imp like a duck to water, and ran away with the 250cc race, doing 21 instead of the 14 laps in the hour-long race. By 1930 he'd earned himself a New Imperial works ride, and his twin sisters, Joan and Thelma, had also become motorcyclists. Still only 15, they used to ride to school every day on a couple of identical

No ropes to keep the crowds under control in those days.

"IT WAS A TOUGH RACE BAPTISM, BUT THE YOUNG MAN SHOWED POTENTIAL, AND AT THE END OF A MUDDY DAY'S SPORT HE PROUDLY RETURNED TO HIS PETERSFIELD HOME WITH A TROPHY"

In a hurry at Imola in 1953, on the 500cc Cammy Norton.

Workshop action with Ron Hankins, preparing the works Norton.

Ariel Colts, and the same year they took an Atom JAP to Brooklands and cracked all the world's records from 50km to 100 miles on the little 98cc bike. The following year dad was mounted on a works Velocette, and became only the third rider to win a gold star for a 100mph lap on the 350 at Brooklands. Away from the banked autodrome he rode in his first TT, in which he finished a creditable 11th on a 350cc supercharged Velocette; this a bike which later earned the name of 'Whoffling Clara,' and my dad the nickname of 'the Aldershot flyer.' It became a legend that at Brooklands dad and Clara would either win the race by a mile or blow up."

Throughout the 1930s the Aldershot flyer chalked up numerous race wins, including the first 100mph lap on a 250 at his favourite, Brooklands. He also held the eight-lap 250 record at Donnington Park, and along with Stanley Woods and Ted Mellors was a member of the Velocette team that scooped the manufacturers' team prize in the 1937 senior TT. In fact, 1937 was a memorable year, as it wasn't just the Aldershot flyer who was winning races; his eight-year-old son –

confusingly also named Les – was soon emulating his father's natural ability on two wheels.

"I was brought up surrounded by the machines of the day, and the smell of Castrol R wafting up into the flat above the garage where granddad Jim and dad would be preparing bikes for another visit to Brooklands, either for a race meeting or yet another attack on some speed record, so it was perhaps inevitable I would become a motorcycle racer. Prewar, a lot of clubs ran motorcycle gymkhanas, and in one organised by the local north Hants club I rode a two-speed 100cc Excelsior two-stroke in a race against another lad, who was driving a miniature racing car. I managed to win, but in my second race I got knocked off and burnt my leg on the hot exhaust pipe, so that was the end of my racing career until the scramble at Elvetham in the spring of 1946."

With the world at war, motorcycle sport was put on hold until 1946, but, with the huge army camp just down the road, there was no shortage of work for the Archer's motorcycle business. During the five

Archer and Lundell coming in to land.

Waiting for the start gate to drop at the Italian GP, 1957.

"DAD WAS MOUNTED ON
A WORKS VELOCETTE,
AND BECAME ONLY THE
THIRD RIDER TO WIN
A GOLD STAR FOR A
100MPH LAP ON THE 350 AT
BROOKLANDS"

An unusual shot of Les on the Norton, taken in July 1958.

war years the shop was taken over by the MoD and virtually turned into a mini-factory, reconditioning all sorts of despatch riders' bikes and making new ones, too. A man who would later play such an important part in the young Archer's racing career also joined the company: his name, Ron Hankins. A useful scrambler and clever engineer, Ron would later fabricate and tune all of the future champion's race bikes, beginning with a 250cc MOV Velocette – a bike that, as Les recalled, earned him a place in the south versus north team in his first season of racing.

"Although there was no racing in the five war years, dad's bikes were occasionally fired up, and thanks to the special 'green oil' granddad used in the engines they were in perfect condition when competition started again in 1946. Brooklands was never used again after the war, but, in the Isle of Man and on the short circuits, dad was soon back on the pace on the New Imperial and the two Velocettes. I was keen to start racing myself, so granddad sorted me out an ex-WD 350cc Matchless to race at the north Hants club scramble. I surprised myself by winning a trophy, but obviously I didn't impress Ralph Venables, who wrote in his notes 'LR Archer won the award for the best performance by a rider under 20 years of age, but he seems to have no future as a scrambler!'"

Les may not have initially impressed Venables, but Ron Hankins could see he was a champion in the making, and it wasn't long before the long hours in the workshop and guidance from his mentor on their private practice track reaped rewards.

"Ron was quick to see that, despite its handling deficiencies, the 250cc MOV Velocette had a lot of potential, and he started experimenting with different frames. As standard the little Velo had a rigid frame, so he fitted rear suspension – something which in the late 1940s was viewed with great suspicion – and we took it to nearby Hungry Hill for testing. This was military land, but granddad obviously knew all the right people as we got permission to use it, and it was the

perfect place to try out all of Ron's new ideas. The seals soon blew on the standard Velocette legs, which resulted in the chain jumping the sprocket, so after a lot of head scratching he got hold of a pair of McCandless units and he made his own internals, which transformed the little Velocette."

Allied to Archer's superlative riding skills, there was barely a grasstrack or scramble during that first season when the Hankins-prepared bike wasn't first past the post, and Les was quickly becoming the man to beat on the potent 250. Before the season was over he was in the south team in the annual race against the north, and was also showing a lot of promise on the tarmac. He made his debut in the TT, where there was an Archer representative in all three international races and the clubman event. The young Les had an inspired ride to finish third on the 250cc MOV in the 250 clubman, while in the lightweight TT his father – 'the Aldershot flyer' – brought the now ageing New Imperial into a superb fourth.

Two great rides, but better was to come later in the week when Bob Foster rode a Velocette from the Aldershot stable into first place in the international junior, rounding off a superb TT for the Archers. By September, the Foster 350 and his father's New Imperial were prepared for Les to race in the Manx, but it was a poor week for the 18-year-old. After smashing a big end at the end of practice on the New Imp, he had to qualify on an EMC, which lasted less than a lap in the 250cc race, and was the leading 350 when the engine blew up at Ramsey on lap four of the senior. A poor week in the island, but before the season was out he rode the Joe Erlich bike to victory in the Hutchinson 100 handicap race, on the perimeter track at Dunholme Lodge in Lincolnshire. His name appeared on the prestigious trophy 14 years after his father had won the same race on his 350cc Velocette. Heady days for the young Archer on the tarmac, but his first love was in the rough and tough world of scrambling, where the 250cc Hankins-prepared Velocette had gone through several incarnations.

"After I left Church's college I naturally joined the family business, and learnt a lot from working with Ron preparing and modifying the scrambles bike. He was an extremely clever and meticulous man, but his secret of success was 'Never alter two things at once, otherwise you don't know what you've done.' During the time I raced the Velocette I guess we tried out half a dozen different frames, and much of what we learnt at this time would hold us in good stead for the future. Ron prepared both the scrambles and road race bikes, but, because my dad was a prewar works racer, the press of the day naturally assumed that they were prepared by the factory, and he (Ron) never received the kudos he deserved for the track successes. Dad and I raced together in the Isle of Man in both '47 and '48, but I quickly realised I was never going to be his equal on the tarmac. I recall I broke down at Ramsey in 1948, and was sat on the side of the road when I heard a bike approaching. It was absolutely flat out, and where most riders were backing off on the throttle this one held it wide open and flew through the bend, and I watched open-mouthed as my father shot past with his handlebars flicking the grass on the wall!"

Like his great pal Mike Hawthorn, Les' national service was deferred until he was 20, but the army quickly acknowledged his prowess on two wheels, and 1950 saw him on the road to Italy and the international six-day trial.

"Along with Eddie Dow I went to Boredon where we were chosen for the army team for the 1950 ISDT, and after testing we went

The flag has dropped, and already Les is in the lead at the 1962 Italian GP.

"THE ARMY QUICKLY ACKNOWLEDGED HIS PROWESS ON TWO WHEELS, AND 1950 SAW HIM ON THE ROAD TO ITALY AND THE INTERNATIONAL SIX-DAY TRIAL"

More action from Imola in 1962.

off to the BSA factory at Small Heath, where they presented us with our bikes: brand new Gold Stars. We modified them to suit each rider, fitted them with twin cables, and three weeks before the ISDT we went to Trieste for final testing. They all ran well, which left us pretty confident of our chances in the event proper, but on arrival in Varesse for the start of the six days BSA presented us with new bikes. Despite our protests that ours were fine they insisted we use the new ones, which we soon discovered hadn't been properly prepared. Mine broke down when the crankcase filled with oil, and I lost time carrying out a repair – it had been fitted with the incorrect oil filter – but I limped on and eventually managed to get to the finish at Imola."

Road racing only lasted for three seasons until Les went into the army, but there was little interruption to his burgeoning scrambles career, which, by 1950, had seen him expand his horizons to the near continent.

"I was desperately keen to get into the British Motocross des Nations team, and as I also wanted to race on the continent I needed to get a 500c bike. Thanks to Ron we'd got the 250cc Velocette going really well, so it was fairly straightforward to transfer these modifications onto a 500T Norton, which had a beautiful power delivery and handled extremely well. Basil Hall had already been racing in Europe for a couple of seasons, and in the Easter of 1950 I got my first taste of continental motocross. After competing in the Hants GN at Matchems Park on the Friday, we travelled together to Namur in Belgium on Sunday, and then journeyed on to Oostmalle in Holland for the race on Monday. It was an amazing but extremely tough experience, racing in and out of the trees at the citadel circuit against legendary continental stars like Auguste Mingels, and after the race my hands were red raw with blisters. It was the first time I'd seen Mingels in action, and there was no doubt he was in a class of his own, throwing the huge FN around like it was a baby 250. The 500T Norton didn't have the top speed of the Belgian bike, but it had a superb power delivery, and, thanks to Ron's suspension mods, the handling was the equal to anything else on the track that weekend."

Aboard the 500 Norton Les was soon chalking up wins in both the UK and France – the latter a country where foreign motocross stars were treated like royalty.

"Most of the continental clubs paid us either decent start or prize money, and my immediate impression was how enthusiastic everyone was. After the ravages of the Second World War thousands of fans flocked to see us crazy motorcyclists in action, and in France especially we received an amazing reception. This usually included music in the streets and a meal with the mayor and other civic dignitaries. I quickly discovered that to cover costs it was essential to share the travelling expenses with another rider, so in '51 I teamed up with Eric Cheney. At that time Eric was mounted on a 350cc Ariel, but we later became team-mates, and during the next five or six years travelled thousands of miles together. He was a good rider, and like me he was very aware that virtually all scrambles bikes of the era were overweight and didn't handle or brake too well."

There was no doubt that the Archer 500T Norton both went and handled extremely well, but the pushrod engine had reached the peak of its tuning potential, and to beat Mingels on his super fast FN something special was called for. It was back to the drawing board, and after 18 months' hard work Les gave the new machine a victorious debut at Shrubland Park, in August 1952.

"I loved the long-stroke Norton single, so, as the bore and stroke of the more powerful OHC Manx road racing engine was the same as the 500T, we decided it was our ideal power unit. Ron's frame for the new bike was fabricated from Reynolds 531 tubing, and based on Norton's famous Featherbed, but it featured curved twin front down tubes for clearance of the 21-inch motocross front wheel, and a single upper frame in place of the wide twin tubes. This allowed us to adjust the steering head angle and foot peg location, and his short stubby crossmembers added to the frame rigidity, and massive gusseting reinforced the steering head. Unbeknown to us, Norton also had the same idea of using the Manx motor in a scrambler, and, while we were working away in our workshop, they made 350 and 500cc bikes for their works rider Johnny Draper to test. By August ours was finished, and after lots of testing at Hungry Hill we took it to Shrubland Park, where, despite a poor start, I managed to win first time out. I was convinced that we had a bike capable of beating Mingels' FN, but Ron told me in no uncertain terms that he wasn't going to allow me to go to the continent before he'd made another. This meant the new bike's foreign debut was put on hold while he made a jig and frame number two."

Archer's win at Shrubland gave Norton an insight: when mounted in a sweet handling scrambles frame, its Manx engine had a lot of potential, so Norton invited the Aldershot rider to sample its two 'works' bikes on the Hungry Hill test track – a test ride that left Les bruised, and one of the factory bikes battered and bent.

"My granddad was friendly with Gilbert Smith at Norton, so it was largely thanks to this we got the two factory bikes to test. The 500 was very fast, but the engine was too powerful for a scrambler, and compared to Ron's the handling was rubbish. The wheelbase was about four inches longer than ours, but the frame couldn't contain the power and I ended up looping it, and we returned it to the factory looking very secondhand. It was obvious Norton had a lot of work to do to make it competitive, and, as they were more interested in pursuing Geoff Duke's road racing efforts, they asked us if we would be interested in developing the scrambler under the guise of an official works package. The agreement was that Eric and I would become the official 'works' riders, and although Norton didn't pay us we had unlimited access to all the spares we needed. This was worth its weight in gold, because, as we soon discovered, using a piece of silk stocking as an air filter was pretty useless, and in dusty conditions the Manx engine had a prolific appetite for wearing out barrels and pistons. In that first season it seemed like we were getting through a new Manx cylinder and piston virtually every other week, but things improved when we started using four unit air filters made by Voxe, and later on we paid Mahrle to supply us with a set of aluminium pistons and a special chrome-lined barrel, which lasted a whole racing season."

Motoring around Europe racing a motorcycle might sound like a romantic way of life, but, as Les explained, to reach the top there was a lot of pre-season planning and paperwork, plus many hours spent burning the midnight oil in the workshop.

"We had a map of Europe on granddad's office wall, so around Christmas time when the dates and locations of the Grand Prix were released we could plan out which other events were taking place relatively close by to them. I'd learned a little French, so being able to write to the organisers in their own language helped a lot, and in that first season of racing on the continent I rode in 25 events. In

Memories of a golden era; a heavy landing on the Norton in 1953.

France there could be anything up to 15 international meetings on the same day, and if we planned things properly during the month of May – which included several national holidays – we could get to race at seven different venues. Typically, we kicked the season off in February by driving down to Marseille, where we caught the boat to Algeria before the 'serious' stuff started around Easter time. Although Ron never travelled with us to any of the GPs, he knew instinctively what state of tune the engines needed to be in for the various circuit conditions, and the octane level of the fuel. So, safe in the knowledge that I had a very competitive machine, I could just concentrate on the racing"

Jim Archer was hugely supportive of his grandson's racing career, but only once saw him in action on foreign soil: the 1953 Luxembourg GP, which Les regards as one of his greatest rides.

"Whether it was because granddad was watching I don't know, but I came to the start line really fired up, and from the drop of the flag shot away with Auguste Mingels. We were together side by side, dicing for the lead for virtually the whole race, but I knew my Norton had the legs on the FN, and on the one long straight I managed to overtake and kept him at bay to win by a machine's length. Mingels was a great sportsman, and as we toured back to the pits he threw his bike down and came over and embraced me, saying 'Les, you've got to go for the championship.'"

In fact, 1953 was quite a year for Archer. Not only did he chalk up numerous wins in both national and international events, he was also a member of the winning British Motocross des Nations team in Sweden, where he took the chequered flag 14 seconds ahead of his nearest challenger. Twelve months later he looked set to replicate that win, and was leading when sand got through the air filter and melted on the piston, causing his retirement. But, as he told me, he didn't always see eye to eye with the ACU about representing his country in the Motocross des Nations.

"Unlike the international events, we didn't get paid to represent our country in the team races, which meant we had to cover all our own travelling expenses. As you can imagine, getting to and racing in an event – which was often several hundred miles and a sea crossing from home – took time and money, but any talk of being paid for our efforts was severely frowned on by the ACU."

Despite this, Les continued to ride in the Motocross des Nations team, but that win in Sweden was his only victory. His eyes were now firmly on the 500cc European championship. The title had been won by fellow Brit Johnny Draper in 1955, but Archer had won the French GP that year in impressive style, and he entered the '56 championship full of confidence. However, as he recalled, his season got off to a poor start, and by the beginning of June he was looking for his first points.

"The first three rounds of the '56 championships were a total

disaster for me, with three retirements in a row – front brake failure in Switzerland, cooked plug in Holland, and a prang in Italy – which meant a third of the series had slipped by without me getting a point. My luck then turned, and in quick succession I won in France on June 10th, at Hawkstone Park on July 7th, and in Belgium on August 5th. In those days the championship was awarded on a rider's best four rides, so when I finished second to Draper in Luxembourg, I was only two points below a maximum score. So whatever happened in the last two races, the championship was mine."

In fact, after he'd finished fourth in Sweden, Les rounded the season off in fine style with a win in Denmark, giving him his fourth outright win for a maximum point 500cc European championship title. In 1957, the 500cc class was awarded full 'world' championship status, and Les recalled his first encounter with the riders from behind the Iron Curtain.

"Their riders all arrived together at the first GP in a big converted bus with all of the bikes in a lorry. They'd obviously been given strict instructions not to mix with any of us Westerners, and at the end of practice they disappeared inside their bus and only emerged when the race was due to start. Unbeknown to them, Auguste Mingels had arranged for our mechanics to accompany us to the start, and they held the bikes while we went along and shook hands with them all. This certainly broke the ice, and at the next round they came to us and gave us each a bottle of vodka; sport had won the day over political nonsense."

Mounted in Hankins' sweet handling frame, the loping broad fat power band of the Manx engine perfectly complemented Archer's fluid riding style, and other than a change to a shorter wheelbase frame and Ceriani forks, to accommodate a Ray Petty short-stroke DOHC Manx engine in 1962, the bike remained true to the original design for over 15 seasons of top class racing. Throughout the 1960s, Les was still highly competitive, and continued to race regularly in France. However, in 1966 the decision was made to sell the substantial Norton racing set to San Francisco-based Bryan Kenny – who raced the short-stroke bike for a season in Europe – while Les bought a new 360cc Greeves to race in the UK. Sadly, his plans were thwarted just a month after taking delivery of the Greeves when he crashed a borrowed Triumph Metisse at Tweseldown, breaking a collarbone and a finger. He decided to call it a day, and his retirement in 1967 brought the curtain down on 21 years of top class racing. A truly memorable 21 years, in which the man from Aldershot on his Hankins-prepared Manx Norton became one of scrambling's all time greats.

Many thanks To Les and Claire for their time and hospitality, and for reliving some wonderful memories from a golden era of motorcycling.

CHAPTER 15

At any round of the British 250cc championship during the 1960s you could bet that a screaming two-stroke Dot or Greeves with John Griffiths in the saddle would be battling for the lead, and if the conditions were muddy, the Nantwich rider would usually be first past the flag.

JOHN GRIFFITHS – MASTER IN THE MUD

Our story opens on a cold Good Friday at Matchams Park in 1964. As the starting gate drops, a thick cloud of chalk dust hits the air as a throng of screaming 250s get away for the first race of the Hants Grand National. Other than the two booming works BSAs of Jeff Smith and Arthur Lampkin, the rest of the 38 starters are all mounted on two-strokes. Among them is John Griffiths, a young man from Nantwich making his national debut on his new works Greeves. Griffiths had been poached from Dot at the end of the '63 season, and as the race developed the youngster from Cheshire was soon showing his promise, becoming embroiled in a fierce battle for fifth place with Smith and the works James ridden by Chris Horsfield. It quickly turned into a race dominated by the Thundersley strokers, and at the end of ten tough laps the first four places were filled by the works Greeves quartet of Bickers, Clough, Goss, and Malcolm Davis, with Griffiths a creditable seventh, ahead of Lampkin and his former team-mate John Banks in the saddle of the factory Dot. Later that day, John would finish third behind Bickers and Clough in the 250cc supporting race, and earn a second podium behind his two new team-mates in the second leg of the 250cc motocross, giving notice that, if all went to plan, Greeves and the new Challenger were serious contenders for that year's world championships.

As it transpired, after starting promisingly with a third in the Spanish GP in Barcelona and a fifth in Italy, Griffiths' own title aspirations were brought down to earth in a painful way with a crash and a badly broken collar bone while testing the new Dunlop rear tyre in Switzerland. He would be on the sidelines for three months before being fit enough to race again.

In a career that began in 1958, John was undoubtedly one of the best quarter-litre scramblers of his day, and, but for another injury in '65, he could have become a top star on the world stage. Fifty years on from that memorable day at Matchams Park I met up with the former Dot and Greeves factory rider, and he began by recalling how his love for motorcycling began with an old New Imperial; a bike with no engine.

"My dad had no real interest in motorcycles, but he did have a New Imp, which was used as his transport to and from his work in Crewe. I remember it always had a pool of oil underneath it, and he spent countless hours tinkering with the engine; eventually, however, dad took the motor out and gave the rolling chassis to me. I was only about seven or eight, but with help from my mates I somehow managed to push it to the top of the steep slope at the back of our house, and I

Aviating the Dot at Hawkstone in 1963.

would then tear back down at what seemed like terrific speed while my friends – who were waiting for their turn – cheered me on. We had a family friend who worked at Bill Webster's motorcycle shop, and when I was about twelve he got me a Big 4 Norton which we kept on my uncle's farm. This was a few miles away at Chetley, but I used to go over there virtually every weekend to ride it around the fields, and, bitten by the off-road bug, I couldn't wait until I was old enough to have a go at a proper event. On leaving school at 15 I'd got a job as an apprentice mechanic at Webster's, and it was through Bill I got my first competition machine: a 197cc Dot trials. By giving my wrong date of birth I got to ride in a few trials before my 16th birthday in 1957, but it was scrambling which excited me, and later the same year I rode in my first event. This was our local circuit at Hatherton Hall, and although I have little or no memory of the actual race, I can vividly recall the exhaustion I felt from legging the Dot through a sea of liquid mud, and the feeling of joy in reaching the finish."

The trials Dot would be John's race machine for two seasons; two memorable ones, which saw the Nantwich flyer win his first race and earn an upgrade to expert status. Race fans were quick to recognise that he was a star in the making, and with a change of machine for the '59 season, Griffiths and his new Francis Barnett became the pairing to beat in the Cheshire centre. He takes up the story again.

"The Franny B was much quicker then my old Dot trials iron,

and with all of the lessons I'd learnt from watching top centre riders, I suddenly discovered I was able to pass people I'd previously struggled to keep in my sights, and I started winning races. Working in Bill Webster's meant that I could do all of my own engine maintenance, but sadly the single front downtube on the Barnett frame wasn't really up to the job, and I had several retirements through breakages. They supplied me with two new frames, but little or nothing was done to address the underlying fault, which was extremely frustrating. So I decided to contact Mr Bernard Wade at Dot. I asked him if there was any chance of a works bike, and much to my surprise he said 'John, you're going to be a top rider,' and readily agreed to let me have one of the latest production 250s, along with a deal which allowed me to have 50 per cent off all of the spares and parts I might need for the 1960 season."

Bernard Wade's faith in the young Griffiths was fully justified, as first time out he won the opening 250 race, and was second in another. However, a 'coming together' in the unlimited race saw the bike returned to Manchester minus its front wheel.

"Jack Matthews and I were heading for the same line through a corner, and as neither of us was prepared to give way we collided and all of the spokes were ripped out of my front wheel. I thought that Mr Wade would be displeased, but his reaction was to say nothing, and he immediately promoted me to the full works team alongside Pat Lamper, Ken Messenger, and Alan Clough. This gave me a chance to compete in all of the rounds of the 250cc British championships, and with Dot handling all of the entries it meant that I could concentrate on fettling and racing the bike. Other than the M1 there was no other motorway, so travelling to events in Kent, Hampshire, East Anglia, or the West Country took hours, but it was great to race on different circuits against the likes of Bickers, Mike Jackson, and the Sharp brothers on their factory Greeves. Although both were powered by similar Villiers engines, their bikes were quite a bit lighter which gave them a top speed advantage, but our Dots handled extremely well, and what we lost on the long straights we could usually make up for in the corners. It made for some fantastically close racing, but riding the bike flat out gave the gearbox an incredibly hard time, and at most meetings I spent the time between heats and final replacing a sheared cog or two."

The now-yellowed pages of press cuttings from 1960 and '61 in John's scrapbooks recall scores of these epic battles between the Greeves and Dot two-strokes, and if the conditions were muddy then Griffiths would usually be first past the flag. At the insistence of Bernard Wade, the bikes allocated to the works riders were to the same specification as the production models, but by the end of '61 they had fallen behind the Thundersley opposition, and even with the top trio in the saddle it was obvious that, to stay in touch, a new lightweight was required. It had to be more powerful, lighter, and have even better suspension than that which Dot had previously developed, and after months of testing by Pat Lamper the new 250 was launched, in January 1962. With a staggering weight saving of 35lb and a 25 per cent performance increase over the previous model, it was obvious that Dot had produced a potential winner, and after Clough and Lamper had ridden it to first and second in 250 and 500cc races at Mansfield in February later that month, it was Griffiths' turn to turn on the magic. In foul weather, not only did he beat the normally unstoppable Clough, but also Jeff Smith and John Burton on their works BSAs, Vic Eastwood, and Joe Johnson to win the 250cc race, and then the 'race of the day' for 500cc machines. The opposition sank without trace in the deep Lancashire mud. The new

In the Spanish sun in his Grand Prix debut, on the works Dot.

"RIDING THE BIKE FLAT OUT GAVE THE GEARBOX AN INCREDIBLY HARD TIME, AND AT MOST MEETINGS I SPENT THE TIME BETWEEN HEATS AND FINAL REPLACING A SHEARED COG OR TWO"

Concentrating very hard to keep ahead of Dave Bickers.

Off-Road Giants!

Dot – named the 'Demon' after it was tested by Dave Curtis for *MCN* – carried Griffiths to numerous victories during the long hot summer of '62. A memorable one for the Nantwich rider, which saw him beat a field of 105 to win the 250cc Irish championship at Downspatrick, and, after a season-long battle with the Greeves ace Bickers and his Dot team-mate Clough, he finished runner-up in the 250cc ACU Star. His chances of lifting the crown were scuppered at the last round at Cuerden Park in October, when the previously reliable engine on the 'Demon' suffered a major blow-up, leaving Griffiths a spectator as Bickers rode to victory and the title. The winter time also saw John notch up a win in a TV scramble, but, disguised by a donkey jacket, he left even Murray Walker struggling to identify the mysterious rider mounted on a 250cc Cotton. This was a victory that, as John recalled, was not met with joy by Bernard Wade, but also one that earned him a much-needed second string machine.

"In practice for the TV scramble my bike went sick, and as there was no time to sort it out Cotton's development engineer and works rider Fluff Brown offered me the use of his spare bike for the race. I guessed that Bernard Wade wouldn't be too happy to see me racing one of the opposition's bikes, so I disguised myself with a hooded donkey jacket. At the drop of the gate I got a great start, but this led to lots of problems for the commentator, Murray Walker, who had no idea who it was in the lead. I won the race, but a couple of days later I received a stern letter signed by MR Wade saying 'Don't do it again or else!' I apologised, but I informed him that I only had one bike, and as this had packed up in practice what other option did I have? Needless to say, from then on I was always supplied with a back up machine."

For the 1963 season Clough was lured away to race a factory Greeves, and John had a new team-mate in the form of John Banks. It would be this duo who would take the name of Dot to the world stage. John takes up the story again with some memories from those early trips to Europe.

"John and I were keen to compete against the best in the world, but when we suggested it to Bernard Wade he poured cold water on the idea, and we were left to sort out the entries and fund the trips ourselves. Our first GP of the '63 season was in Spain, and after meeting up at his house at Bury St Edmunds the pair of us – along with journalist Chris Carter, our new bikes, spares, and riding gear all jam-packed into John's Vauxhall estate car – made the long trip down to Barcelona. The circuit itself was built on an old golf course, and with international motocross something new in Spain, the race day attracted a huge crowd. It was the first time we'd had the opportunity to race against the likes of Torsten Hallman on his championship winning Husqvarna or the factory CZs ridden by the Eastern bloc riders Vlastimil Valek and Victor Arbekov and although we both had decent rides our Dots – which were new bikes off the production line – were hard pressed to keep up. They were no better when we rode at the next GP in Italy – the power was all wrong, and they struggled to climb some of the steep hills – so before the third round in France we took them back to the factory for some remedial tuning. They were returned to us just in time to test ride them around the Banks family orchard, and although they still seemed to be very flat, we had no other option than to load them up and hope for the best. In fact, we quickly discovered in practice the work that Mr Wade had done advancing the port timing had transformed the power characteristics of the engine; it had given us another 3bhp, which meant

that our bikes were now as quick as the fastest Greeves, and at least we could be competitive."

Throughout the '63 season both Griffiths and his team-mate registered regular top ten finishes in the GPs; some impressive performances, which, during the following winter, had both Bultaco and Greeves vying for the signature of the 22-year-old.

"I was now working at Bostock's garage, and several times during the latter part of 1963 I'd had phone calls from Derry Preston-Cobb at Greeves, asking if I would be interested in riding for them the following year. During the winter I also had one from the journalist Peter Howdle to say that Bultaco were interested in me, and they had arranged for me to fly to Barcelona to test the latest factory motocrosser. On arrival I was met by Oriol Bulto, who introduced me to the company MD, John Grace, and later he took me to the family ranch where we rode some practice sections on their latest 150cc trials bike. The following day I had a tour of the busy Bultaco factory – where my lasting memory is of a huge pile of expansion chambers piled high in a courtyard – and then we travelled by train to San Sebastian to their motocross test track. I was impressed by their new bike, and was ready to sign on the dotted line when out of the blue I received another call from Preston-Cobb saying 'Don't sign until you've spoken to me.' I returned to England and spoke to 'Cobby,' who invited me to go to Thundersley to test the new Challenger with Dave Bickers. At the end of a dozen or so laps we pulled up and he – Cobb – asked Bickers why he hadn't passed me, to which Dave smiled and said 'I couldn't.' With that Preston-Cobb produced a contract and I was signed to be an official Greeves works rider, to compete in all of the British and world championship rounds, for which I was paid £300 in three instalments."

As was proven at the Hants Grand National, it didn't take Griffiths long to get used to the handling characteristics of the Challenger, but sadly, the crash in Switzerland brought a promising season to an early end.

"I was pleased with my third in Barcelona and fifth in Italy, and with the muddy conditions I was feeling pretty confident for a good position at the next GP in Switzerland. We went out in the first practice session with my bike fitted with one of the new Dunlop soft-wall rear tyres, and although it cut through the deep mud okay, it certainly didn't like the heavy landing when I jumped the bomb hole. The ground was like ice and I got spat off; I hit the ground hard, and a few minutes later I was in an ambulance on my way to hospital to have my shattered collar bone pinned. I then had to spend three frustrating months waiting for the bones to knit together, and by the time I was fit enough to ride again at Glastonbury I'd missed most of the season. I figured that Greeves might not want to resign me, and agreed with James to test ride their new Starmaker-engined 250. However, before this happened I had another call from Preston-Cobb who croaked over the phone 'Don't sign a contract.'"

Throughout 1964 the Greeves Challenger had been plagued with gearbox problems, but, despite having this replaced with a more robust Albion set of gears, the Thundersley two-strokes were finding it hard to deal with the CZ ridden by Joel Robert – a machine that Griffiths got to both closely examine and later ride on Bickers' test track.

"The Czechs were very secretive as to what made their factory motocrossers both fast and ultra-reliable, so when Joel Robert left one of his spare bikes with Dave Bickers – Dave had agreed to transport it to the next GP – we thought it was the ideal opportunity to give it a

Flying on the works Challenger in a TV meeting at Brill, March 1964.

Leading team-mate Bickers on the mark 2 Challenger in the Belgian motocross GP at Hechtel, April 1965.

spin. Riding it was a revelation; not because it was much quicker than our factory Greeves, but the seamless way it picked up on the throttle, and the superb – bulletproof – gearbox. The Challengers handled well enough – Dave's had a set of Cerianis while I preferred the banana forks – but we had lots of fuelling problems with monobloc carb, and although we carried out lots of tests with Amal the improvements were only marginal, which meant that in a race while our engine was stuttering and not picking up cleanly, the CZs would fly past us in mid-air."

Beset by gremlins, neither Bickers or Griffiths were able to mount a serious world title challenge in '65 – a season that saw John's Grand Prix racing career and his Greeves works ride come to a premature end with a heavy crash and another nasty injury in Czechoslovakia. He takes up the story again.

"I can remember little about the actual crash, but recall waking up in hospital and being told I had smashed my leg and had snapped the main ligament in my knee. It was months before I was able to walk again, but I wanted to continue scrambling, so I bought a special strap with metal plates to help support my knee, and thanks to Bernard Wade I had one of the latest 'White Strength' works Dots for the new season. From my first race in an event near Preston my knee ached like hell, and I knew I wouldn't be strong enough to compete in the GPs again, but thanks to the metal support I was optimistic I could be still competitive.

"Throughout my career I had always raced 250s, but big bore two-strokes were now making their mark in the previously four-stroke dominated 500cc class, and, in an attempt to keep in touch with the opposition, Dot's Phil Bright had fitted a 360cc side port Maico engine into one of their frames for testing. I was immediately impressed by the way the big stroker both performed and handled, and in one of my early races on it I managed to keep Jeff Smith and his world championship wining BSA at bay in the Lancashire mud. Bernard Wade was keen

to make some replicas, but before this could come to fruition Maico changed their engine to a central port, which meant that Dot had to make a new twin downtube frame. For whatever reason this just didn't handle the same way as the single tube original, and only a handful of complete bikes were ever produced before they gave up on the idea. I'd retired from the GPs, but I continued to race in all of the important meetings in the UK, and also went to Spain to compete in three big internationals with my new Dot team-mate John Done. My lasting memories of these are of winning one of the internationals against some top-line Swedes in Santander, and between races getting badly sunburnt in Barcelona."

That win in Santander would be Griffiths' final international win. At the end of the 1967 season he decided to finally call it a day, and his helmet and scrambles gear were hung up for the last time. His retirement brought the curtain down on the scrambling career of one of the best quarter-litre racers of his generation, but as one door closed for John Griffiths, another one soon opened. Having briefly sampled short circuit road racing in the early '60s, he not only returned to the northern tracks of Croft, Aintree, Oulton Park, and Mallory on his Greeves Silverstone, but also raced for four years in the Isle of Man on the same bike, and later a 350cc Oulton and a Bultaco-framed Yamaha. In the lightweight Manx Grand Prix he showed that his racing talents weren't just limited to the rough stuff, and after registering a creditable 13th place on his 250cc Silverstone on his debut ride in 1967, he followed up a DNF in '68 with two impressive second places on his Yamaha in both 1969 and '70. However, at the end of that final lightweight Manx, John decided it was time to call it a day, and he never raced a motorcycle again. For the thousands of fans who lined the scramble tracks in that golden era, the sight and sound of John Griffiths and his screaming Dot and Greeves two-strokes will never be forgotten, and, but for those two cruel injuries, who knows the heights he could have achieved?

On the 360cc Maico-engined Dot, keeping Jeff Smith at bay.

"I CAN REMEMBER LITTLE ABOUT THE ACTUAL CRASH, BUT RECALL WAKING UP IN HOSPITAL AND BEING TOLD I HAD SMASHED MY LEG"

On the Greeves Oulton in the 1968 Manx Grand Prix.

Gordon goes for a works dab in the 1963 Cotswold Cup trial. (Courtesy Gordon Francis)

After a highly successful trials career, Gordon turned his attentions to the world of scrambling, where he quickly became a star. For ten years he travelled Europe, earning his crust racing a 360cc Husky, and in 1969 was crowned Rothmans Champion of Australia and New Zealand.

CHAPTER 16

GORDON ADSETT – A TRAVELLING MAN

The history books record that, back in 1955, Hollywood actor James Dean was killed in a car crash; there was a riot at an Elvis Presley concert in Jacksonville, and the UK was brought to a standstill with a national rail strike. In the motorcycling world John Draper was crowned European 500cc motocross champion; West Germany scooped the trophy in the ISDT, and Geoff Duke scorched his works Gilera around the island at 97.93mph, while down in Surrey a 16-year-old lad was competing in his first trial. His name was Gordon Adsett, although as he rode his 197cc James to the start on that cold winter morning, little could he have imagined that this would be the beginning of a long and highly successful competition career; one in which he would become one of the best all-rounders of his generation.

Gordon was one of that rare breed of men who was equally talented in his old crumpled cap riding against the best in a national trial, or with the front wheel of his Husqvarna clawing the air at an international motocross meeting. Amazingly, 55 years on from that first event, he is still thrilling the classic racing crowds with his all-action riding style. I was lucky enough to meet up with him at the bi-annual 'Down Memory Lane' gathering in Barnstaple, where he relived some of those six golden decades. He began by telling me

how, in the early '50s, a trip on his uncle's BSA ignited a passion to race a motorcycle.

"My dad had no interest in motorcycling, but my uncle owned a BSA Gold Flash, and when I was about 12 or 13 he took me to watch the speedway at nearby Harringey. The sight, sounds, and smell from the bikes was incredible, and I was hooked. Sadly, in those days there was no schoolboy motorcycle sport, so I had to content myself with racing in cycle speedway until I was 16 and old enough to get my first bike. This was a 350cc BSA which I paid £12 for, but I soon swapped it for a 197cc James rigid trialer from Minear and Bruce in Guildford. At that time I had no idea what a trial or scramble was, and only bought the bike because it was a bit like a speedway bike with a big fat rear tyre.

"One of the mechanics asked me if I would like to go and watch a trial, so on the weekend of the Gott Memorial event I rode to the nearby Rising Sun Inn to see what it was all about. Some of the first people I saw were Jimmy Robb on his home-made JMR – Jimmy later went to the States to work for Bud Ekins – Derek Cranfield, BSA-mounted Graham Beamish, and a chap in a cap and long coat who seemed to know everyone; I later discovered this was the journalist Ralph Venables.

Negotiating a narrow stream in the 1963 Knut. (Courtesy Gordon Francis)

Off-Road Giants!

**Gordon (11) battling with Dave Gladwin at Leighton in March 1964.
(Courtesy Gordon Francis)**

"After watching a few sections I decided that trials looked like a lot of fun, so I joined the local Weyburn club and a couple of weeks later I entered my first event. This was a Thames Ditton club trial, and I surprised myself by having quite a good ride – I finished runner-up in the novice class, beaten by just five marks."

The young Adsett's potential was there for all to see, and it only took five trials for him to be upgraded to the experts class; a steep learning curve, because, as he recalled, there was plenty of top class opposition in the south eastern centre, including Don Smith, Gordon Jackson, and 'visiting' stars like Jeff Smith and Eric Adcock, who were both stationed in the army camp at nearby Borden.

"At that time I couldn't afford a car or a van, so for the first three or four seasons I was forced to ride my bike to the trials, which meant I was limited mostly to local club and open to centre events, although sometimes I managed to cadge a lift from Comerford's Reg May, who lived about four miles away. I learnt a lot from watching the likes of Smithy and Eric Adcock, and, after switching to a new 197cc Cotton, I started to pick up a few open to centre awards, which earned me some support from the Gloucester factory. The same season, I was selected to represent the Weyburn club in the centre team trial at Brands Hatch, but I realised that, if was going to improve, I had to widen my horizons and tackle some of the big nationals. My first was the Wye Valley, which I went to with Bob Golner, and after the open to centre trials the severity of the sections was a bit of a shock. I vividly recall one called Middle Cwm, which at the time looked horrendous, and I couldn't believe that anyone could ride it feet up, but of course some of the aces made it look all too easy.

"I missed quite a bit of the 1958 season with bronchial pneumonia, but by the following winter I'd secured a first class award in the Mitchell, and it felt like a major breakthrough. By this time my brother, Derek, was riding and this certainly gave me an all important extra competitive edge, especially when he started beating me."

Four years his junior, Derek began his trials career on an ex-Bill Faulkner Vale-Onslow Francis Barnett, and from the outset looked a natural. He was quickly upgraded to the expert class, and the sibling rivalry acted as a spur to Gordon, with both Adsett brothers regularly featuring in the results of southern-based events. In a shared van, they were now spreading their wings to the trade-supported nationals in far away Devon and Derbyshire, although, as Gordon recalled, this was not without incident or drama.

"For a while we had a 10cwt Bedford three-speed van, which, in October 1961, we drove to Devon for the West of England. I had a good ride, and was pleased to be included in Max King's after-trial radio report, when he told the listeners that 'Gordon Adsett was the only rider to clean Shortway section.' However, I wasn't quite so pleased when, on the journey home, the van broke its axle. We managed to borrow a rope from fellow competitor Bill Martin and got a tow as far as Sparkford, where we parked overnight in a lay-by. The following day, we off-loaded the bikes and rode to Shepton Mallet to compete in another trial, and I think we eventually arrived back home around midnight, just as the semi-floating hub and wheel fell off! We pensioned it off and then got a Morris 1000 pick-up from Peter Stirland, and also got a couple of Comerford Cubs, which were two brilliant little bikes."

For the next two seasons the names of G or D Adsett and their Comerford Cubs featured regularly in the results of major trials, but Gordon was frustratingly denied a premier award in a national event. However, as he recalled, he came agonisingly close in the Mitcham Vase.

"The Mitcham was one of the most important in the south east, and counted towards the ACU's prestigious trials star, which was the forerunner to the British championship. Towards the end of the '62 event, Derek and I were riding around together, and as we arrived at the last section we were tying for the premier. This was a very muddy climb, and after walking it I went first, but footed; however, learning from my mistake, Derek went clean, and won the trial by one mark. It was very frustrating to be beaten by a single dab, but, strangely enough, it did a lot for my confidence, as I'd always considered him to be the better rider, and getting so close to winning gave me a whole new belief in my ability to compete with the best."

This new confidence soon brought its rewards, with first class awards in many of the important nationals, and the offer of a works Greeves. Gordon later discovered that the man with the hat and long coat he had seen at the start of the Gott Memorial trial back in 1955 – Ralph Venables – had recommended him for the factory ride, and he recalled some of the highlights from the next three winter seasons on the Thundersley two-strokes.

"It was quite a surprise when Derry Preston-Cobb approached me with the offer of a works machine; it's not every day you get the chance of having a free bike with factory support, so, as you can imagine, it wasn't a difficult decision to make. They were a great little company to ride for, and the agreement with Cobby was that they supplied the bike and spares, and also paid for my entries and expenses to compete in the trade-supported nationals. At that time they were supporting a huge numbers of trials and scrambles riders, which meant that Bill Brooker and his team in the competition department were always working flat out keeping all the works bikes in tip-top condition. By then I'd been working as a mechanic in the Victoria motor works in Godalming for six years, so I did all my own engine preparation work and fettling,

Gordon (69) dicing for the lead at Tweseldown. (Courtesy Gordon Francis)

"HE WAS QUICKLY
UPGRADED TO THE EXPERT
CLASS, AND THE SIBLING
RIVALRY ACTED AS A SPUR
TO GORDON"

and the only time my bike went back to the factory was before a major event like the Scottish."

The records reveal that in the early '60s Gordon had some superb rides in the Scottish Highlands, and never finished lower than 14th on the 250cc Greeves. He also had some memorable performances in two of the trials world's other important events: the Scott and the British experts, the latter of which he came very close to winning in both 1964 and '65.

"Bob Golner encouraged me to have a go at the Scott time and observation trial – described by him as 'a great day's sport' – but it was just my luck that both years I competed it poured with rain. The course across the moors was about 80 miles, with 70 observed sections, but the mud was horrendous, and in my first ride only around 40 out of the 185 starters managed to finish. Sammy Miller won on his 500cc Ariel, and I was pleased to get the best newcomer award just ahead of John Banks, who was also riding in his first Scott. We were told it was the most difficult conditions ever in the trials then 50-year history.

"The '64 event was the second time I'd qualified for the British experts, and against a line-up which included the likes of Sammy Miller, Scott Ellis, and Mick Andrews, I was probably classed as one of the underdogs. This was perfect for me, as it meant I could just treat the sections like those in an ordinary open to centre event, with no pressure to do anything extra special. I also had total confidence in my works Greeves, which, thanks to some modifications I'd done to the porting and a different Amal carburettor, was creating a lot more bottom end torque, making it perfect for the slippery conditions."

The combination of Adsett and the Thundersley two-stroke was an ideal one, and at the end of a tough day's sport Gordon finished runner-up to Sammy Miller on the works Ariel, ahead of a galaxy of the trials world's best. To prove it was no one-off fluke, 12 months later he piloted the works Greeves to third in the same event – won by Scott Ellis ahead of Miller's Bultaco – but the British experts would be one of only a handful of trials for him in 1965. He was by now an expert scrambler, and his win in the Sidcup Sixty club's Young's Challenge Cup – the opening round of the south eastern centre championship – would be one of his last on the trials Greeves, as he would soon be bound for Europe and the life of a professional motocross rider.

"The progression from trials to scrambling seemed like a natural one, so with the money I got from selling the Comerford Cub I bought myself a 250cc Greeves motocrosser. I managed to win a couple of novice finals at Tweseldown, but the Greeves wasn't very reliable so I bought a 500cc Tribsa from Brian Fowler and by the end of my first season I was upgraded to an expert. I was now firmly smitten by the scrambling bug but quickly realised that if I was going to be competitive in the experts class I needed a new bike, so during the winter of 1964-'65 built myself a Triumph Metisse. Thanks to the help I received from Mick Mills, his father, and Derek, the bike – with its fast and robust pre-unit Triumph engine, Rickman frame, Ceriani forks, and 7R brakes – went, handled and stopped extremely well, and at the time I thought it was the bee's knees."

With a top class machine Gordon was soon on the pace, and before the 1965 season was out he'd been selected to ride for the south east at the annual team scramble at Cadwell Park, and, thanks to a fine third behind Andy Lee and world champion Jeff Smith in the Lincolnshire Grand National, he qualified for his international licence.

"I'd ridden in a couple of trials in France – including the St Cucufa, where I'd finished third behind Roy Peplow and Sammy Miller – and this had really whetted my appetite to race there. At that time I was working at Comerfords alongside several Americans and Australians who were racing regularly on the continent, and they were earning some good money from their weekend's sport. My third in the Lincolnshire GN was just the break I needed, and, thanks to Ken Heanes – a regular competitor across the channel – I got my first entry accepted, and he and I flew with our bikes from Lydd to Le Touquet for the meeting in northern France. The atmosphere in the host town of Aire-sur-la-Lys was fantastic, and on the morning of the race all the riders and their bikes were escorted through the streets by the local Gendarmes with the instructions of 'Make as much noise as you can to attract the crowds.' I had a pretty good day on the track, finishing third overall, and returned home with a few francs in my pocket and my head full of plans and ideas for the future. I quickly made my mind up that scrambling in France was a decent way of making a living, and on returning home I spoke to journalist Peter Fraser for some tips on achieving this goal. Peter was an inspiration, and he gave me lots of good advice on how to get the all important carnets for the bike, and how best to secure regular rides with the French clubs. His top tip was to 'write an accompanying letter with your entry form in French,' and from the first race onward this promotional side was organised brilliantly by my brother-in-law Edward Smythe, sister Josephine, and John Trigg – the interpreter – leaving me with the tasks of keeping myself fit, bike maintenance, and racing."

Fraser also advised Gordon that to earn a good name and get regular rides, it was also extremely important to make every effort to turn up at a meeting – something that pushed his mechanical skills to the limit when, bound for Reims a couple of weeks later, the engine of his Thames van blew up in Ashford.

"I was on my way to catch the 9am boat from Dover to Calais when suddenly the engine went bang, and it was obvious that a big end had gone. I limped to a main Ford garage, and, yes, they had a replacement engine, but it was a nine hour job, and as it was a Saturday morning there was no way they could do it in time. I told him I worked as a mechanic, so we set to, and by 1pm the engine was fitted and I was on my way again. Sadly, I missed the next boat to Calais, and the only option was to get the one which went to Dunkerque. We docked at midnight, and with Rennes three hundred miles away I then had to drive all through the night, arriving just in time for practice. The course itself looked like a giant slag heap with lots of man-made jumps, but, despite being tired from driving all night, I had a great day's sport and eventually finished runner-up to Andy Lee. This generated a huge amount of good publicity, which for a relative unknown went a long way to securing me entries the following year."

Gordon began the 1966 season on the Triumph Metisse, but by June he was racing a 360cc Husqvarna two-stroke – not just in England and France, but further afield in Italy, with a memorable trip to communist controlled Yugoslavia. As he recalled, the latter left him with a wad of virtually useless prize money.

"Although extremely fast, the Triumph Metisse was a big heavy lump over the jumps, so in June '66 I secured a 360cc Husky through the importer Brian Leask. Following the advice I'd received from Peter Fraser my continental entries were all accepted, and after three weekends racing in France I journeyed on to Italy and then to

On his way to special first class on his Greeves in the 1964 Scottish.
(Courtesy Gordon Francis)

On the 250cc Greeves at Tweseldown, mid 1960s.
(Courtesy Gordon Francis)

Yugoslavia in my Thames van. With money fairly tight the old van also acted as overnight accommodation in Trieste, where I slept in a car park before the next weekend's meeting in Yugoslavia. I was paid start money which was the equivalent of around £120, but of course little did I realise at the time the Yugoslav currency was virtually worthless, as it was impossible to change once I'd crossed the border back into Italy. I later learned that to get around this the Swedish riders put their money into a local bank account and used it later for a winter's skiing holiday."

After a winter working for Jackson's Renault dealership in Godalming, Gordon spent the whole of the summer of 1967 racing on the continent; the first of ten happy years as a professional motocrosser. During that time, the records show his name on the podium not only in France, but also in Austria, Germany, Switzerland, Belgium, Italy, and a memorable winter down under in 1968-'69 when he was crowned Rothmans champion.

"During the summer season I was based in a caravan near Le Mans, and although I was there on my own the likes of Dave Nicoll, John Banks, Andy Lee, and a host of Finnish riders were frequent visitors. There was some decent money to be made, and typically at a big meeting you could expect to pick up an average of £250 for a win. At the end of the season I returned to the UK and worked for both the Renault garage and also for Ken Heanes, but when I heard about the Rothmans series my brother-in-law Edward wrote to the organisers putting my name forward. For a while we heard nothing, then I got a phone call from Tim Gibbes with the request 'Would you like to come to Australia?' Originally Dick Clayton was pencilled in to go along as part of a three-man international 'three flags' team, with Welshman Randy Owen and the Austrian Alfred Postman, but he had to pull out, and I was his replacement. The agreement was that our bikes would be shipped by sea and the organisers would pay for our round-the-world air tickets, and arrange all our accommodation with local families for the 12-round series, which would take place at various tracks in Australia and New Zealand.

"As you can imagine, it didn't take too long to make my mind up, and at the beginning of October I was bound for Perth in Western Australia. On arrival we discovered the bikes had arrived safely at the Freemantle docks, but actually getting them off the ship took several hours, as the dockers didn't appreciate us interrupting their Friday afternoon game of cards, and it wasn't until Tim Gibbes used some words of persuasion did they release them just in time for the following Sunday's race. Motocross was taking off down under, and not only did it attract some decent size crowds, we soon discovered that Australia's number one Gary Flood was a fierce competitor, and not an easy man to beat. Like nearly all the circuits we experienced over the next months, the track at Herne Hill was very sandy – conditions which I loved – and I won the first round, with Randy a close second on his ex-Bickers CZ. That pretty much set the scene for the rest of the series, which took us all across mainland Australia, to Tasmania, and finally on to New Zealand in February."

Despite the strong home opposition, most of the races in the Rothmans series had seen either Gordon or CZ-mounted Owen first past the flag, and going into the final round in New Zealand it was three wins each. It was the championship decider, and from the start the two main protagonists were locked in a wheel to wheel battle. The lead changed several times, but on the last lap the canny Adsett got in front and held his rival at bay to scoop the coveted Rothmans trophy by the narrowest of margins. It was the end of the race series, but not the end of Gordon's world tour, as the next two months would see him lapping up the sun in Fiji and enjoying a lengthy stopover with Bud Ekins in Hollywood, before eventually arriving back in the UK in March for another hard summer's racing.

Scrambling brought its inevitable injuries, and over the years he suffered two broken collarbones, a broken wrist and kneecap, and some major shoulder damage, but he recalled a spill while racing in Italy as perhaps his most spectacular.

"I don't remember much about it, but apparently I went full bore off the edge of a quarry, and when I came round I was lying on the ground looking up at a crowd of people peering down at me from the quarry top. The bike was a bit bent and twisted, but amazingly I got up and walked away without a scratch on me."

The occasional crashes did little to deter Gordon's determined riding style, and the early '70s saw numerous meetings with him wearing the winner's garlands. 1972 was perhaps his best season, winning nine meetings outright, which made him the most successful non-domestic rider in France that year. It was a great life, but Gordon was acutely aware that the career of a professional motocrosser wasn't going to last forever. So, with an eye to the future, in 1973 he enrolled on a three-year diploma course in automobile engineering at Guildford Technical College. He continued to race successfully for the next three years, with many international wins in France, and against the world's best managed a creditable 11th overall in the 1974 250cc Swiss GP. This Grand Prix was his lone appearance in a world championship event; as he rarely raced in the UK, he wasn't on the ACU's grading list.

After passing his exams, Gordon took up a post as lecturer in motorcycle engineering at Merton Technical College, and the end of the 1976 season saw the curtain fall on the Adsett motocross career. With the Husqvarnas pensioned off, he returned to his first love of trials, and on a variety of machines – including Montesa, Yamaha, Aprilia, and Sherco – continued to ride for the next 30 years, still good enough to win the Greybeards event two years on the trot in 2003 and 2004. However, the lure of racing was a strong one, and in 2004, at an age when most men are happy to put their feet up, he returned to the classic scrambles scene on a 380cc CZ. Five years down the line he is still racing with the same verve that made him such a favourite with the crowds back in the 1970s, and the are few classic meetings at home or in France where the name of Gordon Adsett doesn't appear in the results.

Big thanks to Gordon for his time and hospitality, and reliving some wonderful memories from a golden era in off-road sport.

EPILOGUE

I hope that in producing this book I've been able to record in print some of the profiles of the men and women who, back in the 1960s, were my boyhood heroes: it was a glorious era and memories of it will live with me forever.

This is the land of lost content,
I see it shining plain.
The happy highways where I went
and cannot come again.

– A E Houseman

Also from Veloce Publishing –

A fascinating and nostalgic compilation of rider profiles written over a three year period, that originally appeared in *Classic Motorcycle* magazine, now accompanied by a new set of over 100 photographs. This book beautifully captures a much-loved time in motorsport.

ISBN: 978-1-84584-190-4
Hardback • 25x20.7cm • £19.99* UK/$39.95* USA • 128 pages • 115 b&w pictures

For more info on Veloce titles, visit our website at www.veloce.co.uk
• email: info@veloce.co.uk • Tel: +44(0)1305 260068
* prices subject to change, p&p extra

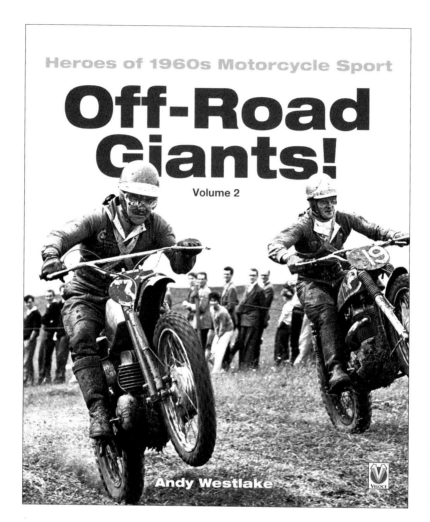

A long-awaited follow-up to the much-loved *Off-Road Giants!* Personal interviews with some of the greats of off-road motorcycling from the 1950s, '60s and '70s, along with some stunning period photographs that paint a wonderful picture of what motorcycling was about in this golden era.

ISBN: 978-1-845843-23-6
Hardback • 25x20.7cm • £19.99* UK/$39.95* USA • 128 pages • 123 b&w pictures

For more info on Veloce titles, visit our website at www.veloce.co.uk
• email: info@veloce.co.uk • Tel: +44(0)1305 260068
* prices subject to change, p&p extra

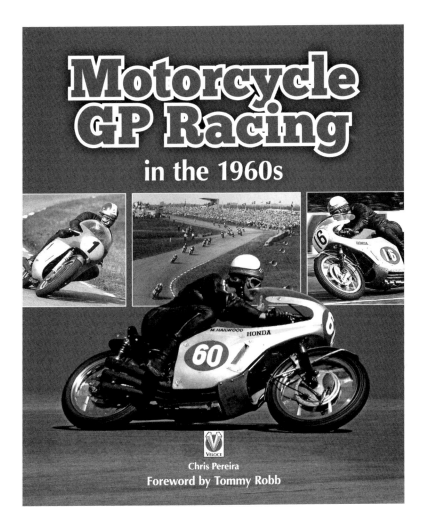

This book examines the classic period of Grand Prix racing from 1960 to 1969, and the men and machines involved. A fascinating exploration of the last decade of 'traditional' Grand Prix racing, before significant events changed the nature of the sport forever.

ISBN: 978-1-845844-16-5
Hardback • 25x20.7cm • £30* UK/$49.95* USA • 176 pages • 177 colour and b&w pictures

For more info on Veloce titles, visit our website at www.veloce.co.uk
• email: info@veloce.co.uk • Tel: +44(0)1305 260068
* prices subject to change, p&p extra

From a race in decline, to the world's most famous and iconic road race, *TT Talking* tells the story of one of the most dramatic eras in the history of the Isle of Man Tourist Trophy. Charlie Lambert tells the story of this sensational upturn, from his own role behind the microphone, to the pressures, controversies, laughs, and sadness that go with being the man at the heart of the world's most famous road race.

ISBN: 978-1-845847-50-0
Paperback • 22.5x15.2cm • £14.99* UK/$24.95* USA • 160 pages • 45 colour pictures

For more info on Veloce titles, visit our website at www.veloce.co.uk • email: info@veloce.co.uk • Tel: +44(0)1305 260068
* prices subject to change, p&p extra

INDEX

127

Off-Road Giants!